The Winter Fens

Edward Storey was born at Whittlesey in the Isle
of Ely and the area has been his home ever since.
He is an established poet and has published five
collections of verse. His writings include *Portrait of
the Fen Country, Four Seasons in Three Countries,
Spirit of the Fens, Summer Journeys Through the
Fens* and *Fen Boy First.*

The Winter Fens

EDWARD STOREY

Illustrated by Helen Hale

ROBERT HALE · LONDON

ISBN 0 7090 5649 4

Robert Hale Limited
Clerkenwell House
Clerkenwell Green
London EC1R 0HT

2 4 6 8 10 9 7 5 3 1

Photoset in North Wales by
Derek Doyle & Associates, Mold, Clwyd.
Printed and bound in Malta
by Interprint Limited

Contents

Acknowledgements

I am particularly grateful to the following for permission to quote from copyright material: A.P. Watt Ltd for *Hills & the Sea* by Hilaire Belloc; A. & C. Black Ltd for *While Following the Plough* by J. Stewart Collis; Faber & Faber Ltd for the *Four Quartets* by T.S Eliot; Miss Norah Hartley for *The Brickfield* by L.P. Hartley; Polly Howat for *Ghosts & Legends of Lincolnshire & the Fen-country* and David Higham Associates Ltd for *The Nine Tailors* by Dorothy L. Sayers.

My thanks are also acknowledged to those people who have allowed me to quote from personal papers, letters or private publications.

Whilst every effort has been made to trace and contact copyright holders prior to publication, there are a few instances where this has proved impossible or no replies were received. Any omissions will be rectified at the earliest opportunity if notified.

for
STEPHEN BRUETON
who shares the pleasures of good books,
good ale and good cricket,
and without whose quiet persuasion
this volume would not have been written.

Introduction

I would forfeit the hearths of many a country
To be stretched on the bleak winds of a land
Where fields are the breast of a much-loved woman
And earth asks of its own no explanation ...

i

If you are fortunate to live in a place where you feel you belong you will know that the landscape of the place has several layers of meaning. As well as its geographical features it becomes an image of a private world where a certain harmony with oneself is experienced as in no other place.

What gives the Fens their particular character is not just the flatness, the space and light which are spoken of so frequently. Equally important are the shadows, mists, floods and blackness of winter. I have met fenmen who are pleased to see a misty day because it diminishes the vastness of the space around them. They need shadows as well as light, a feeling of enclosure as well as freedom. Such opposites are necessary to complete the whole.

Similarly, to love a landscape you must not first ask if it is beautiful, for beauty often is a thing that passes. Nor can you say after an acquaintance of one season, that it is attractive, for brief affections can deceive with age. To love a landscape you must also know its faults and darker moods. You must know it, not only for a year, but for a lifetime. Only then, perhaps, can you say it is the place you most love, the place where you are most contented and at home. It is a familiar maxim but the only one by which we can measure what we mean when talking about that part of the country where we know we belong.

Having made that claim I decided that I had to put it to the test by writing about my own landscape entirely during the winter months. Having done so I think I can say with some confidence that I will stand by what I have written, that I have enjoyed the season as much as any other, if not more so, because so much has been new to me.

But it would be a mistake to see this account as the story of just one winter. Although many of the descriptions come from the season in which I was actually writing, i.e. the winter of 1992/3, they could apply equally to other years in which I have experienced similar conditions. The main difference is in the people I have met and the places I have been to, people who have known many more winters and were prepared to share their memories with me.

Despite whatever hardships the season can bring, I like to believe that winter can also give us many pleasures. It allows some of us to turn our backs on the more tiresome tasks of life. The lawn-mowers have been put away, the gardens left to be turned over by the frost's trowel, and we can draw the curtains early against the darkening sky to enjoy the comforts of an open fire and a good book – or whatever it is we choose for our relaxation.

I suppose the domestic imagery can be too cosy for there is still work to be done, whether it is winter or not. On the farms the cattle must be fed, machinery maintained, men employed, expenses paid, the next crops planned. The farmer may well say that he has no time to sit idly in front of a fire dreaming of summers past, or to come. It is the same with most professions – doctors, teachers, office-workers, shop assistants, postmen and tax-collectors – all might claim that they have as much work to do in the winter as at any other time of the year, perhaps more. Nevertheless, I am sure that part of us does go into a kind of hibernation and we hope for at least some rest from our labours if only as a compensation for the harsh weather we may have to endure.

Personally, I like the seasons to be different and see no point in attempting to contradict nature's intentions. As Shakespeare said in *Love's Labour's Lost*,

> At Christmas I no more desire a rose
> Than wish a snow in May's new-fangled mirth,
> But like to each thing that in season grows ...

It was, no doubt, much easier years ago to separate the seasons than it is today. The year then dictated the pattern of life and most people were compelled to conform, being more helplessly at the mercy of nature than we are now. We seem to delight in competing with nature and do our best to throw the seasons out of kilter. Our winter diet will not necessarily vary all that much from what we eat all the year round. We can have strawberries for Christmas and can move easily from one warm environment to another without feeling the cold blast of winter touch our faces. We have gained benefits that would have been undreamt of by our forefathers, but we have also lost that sense of wonder and novelty that each season used to bring. And yet, who can resist the tinge of excitement that comes with the first light fall of snow? And who can decide which is the more exciting – to see the arrival of the first few flakes of snow in daylight, or to wake up one morning to find the world already quietly and magically white? The aftermath of dangerous roads, of slush and possibly floods, does not concern us at that moment. The beauty of snow is either in its falling or in its unblemished whiteness at dawn – a state of perfection that will not last long but a rare moment that can still bring out the child in us.

What often makes or mars winter is our preparation for it. We can anticipate its pleasures or fear its discomforts. If we allow it to attack us without warning we shall resent it as much as we would an unwelcome guest. To look forward to it in readiness will make its arrival more acceptable, or even bearable. Those of us who still enjoy the satisfaction of a log fire will know, as we sweat over the stubborn saw or axe in April, that it helps to think of the glowing hearth we shall have in December. When the chisel refuses to split the next piece of beech or elm, it sweetens the task to remember the modest pride that will come with the stacking of the logs outside the back door, ready for those fires to come. Although there is sadness in the chopping up of a fallen tree we can take comfort in the new purpose the wood will have when the year comes to its climax. The same is true of the many other jobs we might choose to do, whether it's salting down a ham, bottling fruit, making pickles, or simply clearing out the gutterings or burning the leaves. Winter will be enjoyed more if we make room for it. I like to remember the words of William Blake, 'In seed time learn, in harvest teach, in winter enjoy.'

ii

But when does winter begin? When do we feel that it has arrived? Does it come with the first foggy morning, or the first frost on the grass? Not necessarily, for these deceiving signs can be seen in autumn. Nor should we rely entirely on the calendar, for the seasons themselves can be fickle and disrespectful of official dates. Who can decide on the exact time at which winter will appear? For some the turning back of the clocks is sufficient proof that the long dark months are upon us. For the motorist the beginning of winter is undoubtedly the first morning when the car's windscreen needs de-icing. On the other hand, most farmers will not normally recognize winter until January, whilst a friend of mine is adamant that winter definitely begins on 1 November – All Saints' Day: 'I never eat winter vegetables, like parsnips or Brussels sprouts until that date. It would be preposterous to do otherwise.' We also have Hallowe'en and Guy Fawkes Night competing for the same dubious honour. The date-line, it seems, is moveable, depending on either the weather or our own idiosyncratic attitudes to the season.

For me it is when the stars and planets appear in what I consider to be their correct places in the sky – in those familiar positions where I first learned about them as a boy, when to be out on a dark winter's night was one of life's excitements. It still is. Despite the fact that space is no longer an unconquered mystery, I am unfailingly delighted and reassured by seeing the constellations where they belong. The Plough, Orion, and the Pleiades are never quite the same if seen by chance at some unearthly hour in another season. They are part of winter and, when they have taken up their appointed places, I can relax. More than the first fall of snow, a bright frosty night in November is all I need to believe that winter has arrived.

And where better to see such nocturnal splendour than in the Fens? If that vast space above us gave summer its dome of endless light, now it gives to winter a depth of darkness that is awesome and, in a strange way, just as visible. Against the blackness the planets, stars and distant galaxies open up a universe that makes our tiny earth feel in its infancy. Though it may claim equality in age with many of those remote lights – some of which are already burnt out – the earth still feels young.

So for me, winter magnifies the sky and stretches space to its uttermost. On such a star-lit night the mind can find wings and feel part of something stupendous, unfathomed, timeless.

Yet, how easy it is to forget what darkness is like these days. We are so used to artificial light everywhere – in our towns, cities, villages and houses, that when we come face to face with the natural darkness of a winter sky we can be overwhelmed. I remember an occasion when I was staying with some friends who lived at some distance from civilization, surrounded only by farms and trees. After supper I went outside to look at the sky. It was not a frosty night and the few scattered stars were not immediately visible. But the darkness was and I rushed back into the house, shouting 'Quick! Come and look at the dark!' My friends, no doubt, thought that I had consumed too much wine but I knew my jubilation had not been aroused by an excess of the grape. It was the sudden re-acquaintance with something which our ancestors took for granted. Again, the opposites are necessary for, by the same law, I am quickened by the clear mercurial light of a winter's day.

iii

I appreciate that it is not everyone's favourite season. During the writing of this book I have met many people in their eighties and nineties who dread its approach. As one lady said to me, 'It's not the cold or the wet I mind so much, it's the dark.' Another said, 'I used to like the snow, but not now. I can't abide the cold.' And for many the cost of warmth is seen as an extravagance that they cannot afford.

What I have tried to do in these chapters is to give a balanced view of what life in the winter Fens is like now and what it was like in the past. To achieve this I have talked to farmers, doctors, a country parson, an old fen-skater, and I have sat in a score of houses talking with men and women who have known no other part of England, sharing with them their own memories of winter. I have also visited a farmland museum, the Welney Wildfowl Centre, a fenland brewery that has a 200-year-old history, and I have followed the fund-raising exploits of a male voice choir as it travelled around the towns and villages of Cambridgeshire, giving concerts and entertaining elderly people in care. I have also been able to use some previously unpublished material, particularly in Chapter 11, *Mr John Thompson Remembers*, a superb example of oral story-telling that was preserved in four excercise-books by his son.

What I do know is that this volume could not have been written without the help of several people who were willing to share their knowledge with me. They include Mrs Laura Addison, Mr Trevor Bedford, Mr Hugh Cave, Dr Peter Cave, Mrs Lorna Delanoy, Mr Nigel Elgood, Mrs Polly Howat, Mr Jack Kerridge, Dr Ross Mitchell, Mr Don Revett, the Reverend John Seaman, Mr Percy Wright, the Peterborough Male Voice Choir (and particularly its Secretary, Mr David Ingleby), the museums and libraries in the area, and my publishers. Because of them a fenland winter means even more to me now than it did when I first set out on my enquiry and, through them, I have been able to write about places in the Fens I have not written about before. That in itself has been my reward and I hope something of my pleasure has survived in the written word.

Lastly, my thanks must also go to the publishers and authors whose work I have quoted. A detailed bibliography is given at the end of this book, with my acknowledgements.

E.S. 1993

1   The Wild Swans Return

… Now they drift on the still water,
Mysterious, beautiful;
Among what rushes will they build,
By what lake's edge or pool
Delight men's eyes when I awake some day
To find they have flown away?

W.B. Yeats

i

To see the white swans flying in against an ice-blue sky is to witness one of the most beautiful sights in the winter Fens. To know that those powerful wings have beaten the air for 2,500 miles on their way from Russia to Welney, is to wonder again at the stamina and navigational skills of birds who come each year to winter on our washlands. Their flight, naturally, is made in stages from northern Russia, across Germany and Holland, and many of the swans will arrive at night rather than in broad daylight because they have probably used the stars to guide them. But, whenever they come, and whatever the weather, their advent is a cause for celebration – one which will be repeated each day as they return from their feeding-grounds to the shallow waters they will use for roosting.

The arrival of the wild Bewick's Swans (named after Thomas Bewick) is only part of the spectacle at Welney. Also flying in from Iceland will be the Whooper Swans who will have flown over 1,200 miles from their breeding-grounds in the Arctic to spend a winter in what they hope will be the warmer climate of the English Fens.

From the middle of October to late November the washlands

Now they drift on the still water

expect to receive up to 6,000 Bewick's and 800 Whoopers who will stay until March of the following year. In addition to the migratory swans there are the resident mute swans, mallard, pintail, wigeon, teal, geese, shovelers and pochards – a carnival of wildfowl that will entertain more than 20,000 human visitors during the winter months.

Many of the swans will be returning to feeding-grounds which they have made their own over the years, bringing their new families with them. Some have been coming for up to twenty-five years, amassing a total of 125,000 miles in their lifetime. Their time of arrival will depend very much on the weather and wind direction. Wanting to take advantage of a north wind the Whooper Swans will leave the Arctic Circle as early as October, resting perhaps on the Orkneys or mainland of Scotland before starting the last lap to Welney. The Bewick's Swans will wait for a northeaster to make their flight easier. An aerial view of the washlands at Welney must be, for them, similar to that of a jumbo-jet coming in to land at Heathrow. The long stretch of the Old and the New Bedford rivers look just like runways, and already there is an air of excitement at the Welney Wildfowl Centre as the first birds touch down.

My interest in this aspect of fenland life was encouraged by a meeting with the manager of the Welney Wildfowl Centre, Don Revett, a quiet, thoughtful and dedicated man who belongs to the washlands as much as the birds do. Taking over from the legendary Josh Scott ten years ago, he has seen the popularity of the centre grow in both membership and facilities. Now visitors can have the benefit of a well-stocked shop, tea-room and lecture theatre, as well as the observatory and hides on the Hundred Foot Bank.

I asked Don how many visitors he could expect in a year and was surprised to learn that the number would be in excess of 32,000, with coach parties from Kent, Surrey, Sussex, Nottingham and Lincolnshire in addition to the 10,000 members who come from all parts of the British Isles by car. Despite these statistics 'bird-watching' is still a solitary occupation and you should not expect to get a lively conversation going between 'twitchers'. They are there to watch and one of the essential requirements in watching birds is to be quiet. So it is possible to have a very peaceful day on the Welney washlands, especially if you can be there at times other than weekends or holidays.

Don Revett has the eyes of a washlander. You can see all the seasons, weathers, hopes, disappointments and concern in his eyes. He is part of something bigger than a bit of floodwater in the Fens – large though it is. For him this is where the universe meets. Birds, people, history, events and seasons come within his compass. He spoke to me of that 'magical feeling' when the washlands are covered in fog at dusk, when the wetlands reflect the magnificent colours of sunrise, of when the swans fly into the lagoons under flood – lighting for their evening feeding – and the sadness that is felt when they depart.

I asked how the birds reacted to artificial lighting, to being put 'on show'? 'They love it,' he said. 'It helps them to find their roosting-place for the night and I believe they enjoy their moments of stardom.' It is certainly theatrical.

ii

Welney provided the ideal place of a wildfowl centre, situated as it is in an area where the history of modern Fenland began – that is, after the drainage of the Fens in the seventeenth century. Before Cornelius Vermuyden produced his ambitious plans for draining this neglected part of England, the Fens were made up of vast areas of bogland, meres, reed-beds and untamed rivers pushing their way around the few islands that existed, such as Ely, Thorney, Chatteris, March, Whittlesey, Ramsey and Manea. The waters around these islands offered a plentiful supply of fish, wildfowl and reeds for the daily requirements of local people. Drainage of the Fens would threaten their livelihood and make them vulnerable to outside influences. It is not surprising that fenmen resisted these changes to a landscape that had given them a source of income and security for generations.

But changes were inevitable and the Fens we have today are very different from those before Vermuyden's plans became reality. In fact we should no longer be using the word 'fens' for they do not exist as such. What we call Fens today is the exact opposite of what they were. Now they are fertile, cultivated and, for the most part, dry. Only occasionally, in very wet winters, do we get any idea of what conditions must have been like over three hundred years ago.

Something I did learn from Don Revett was that swans not

only keep together as families but they also have a deep sense of loyalty to a certain place. Several generations of swans have been known to winter at Welney and, by various methods of ringing, records of each family have been established over the years. Many of the birds fit into group names such as 'Darky' 'Pennyface' and 'Yellowneb' but even more surprisingly they also have individual names such as Frappi, Pagle, Burnie, Pedro, Pantile, Band-aid and Lopaz. Often their names are created out of the initials on their rings. If I remember correctly one swan with the initials D.C.D. was named Decadent.

The swans have also learnt how to adapt to modern farming, which helps to supplement their food supply. The machines that lift the potato and sugar-beet crops leave quite a lot of waste on the land and the swans are quick to take advantage of this. They also enjoy nibbling the young green shoots of winter wheat. On the whole farmers do not object to this light grazing which helps to thicken the crop. The main problem in a wet winter is caused by the swans' webbed feet trampling down the crops. A few thousand pairs of feet can soon turn the black fen soil into a paddy-field.

I have been out to the Welney Wildfowl Centre and its hides several times this winter and have seen the vast assembly of birds in rain, sunlight, snow, and freezing wind. Although so many people come to watch the birds it is still a private and solitary pastime, especially in the mornings when the Fens have their own particular quietness. The bleakness of the place can intimidate, it is true. The air is sparse and chilling, raw and penetrating. It gnaws through to the very marrow of your bones. Your eyes water, your feet absorb the cold of centuries and become stone. The sky can be grey and abstract, the water like liquid steel. However it is still exhilarating and worth coming for, for this is a special place on earth where you can feel part of some mysterious, primordial world where only water, land, birds, sky and silence meet to create a world far removed from the noisy, material world that most of us now are compelled to inhabit.

iii

The Welney Wildfowl Centre was officially established in 1970, though Sir Peter Scott had realized its potential as an important 'wetland' forty years earlier. Since then the trust has acquired

more land and now owns a thousand acres of the Bedford Level
washes between the Old and New Bedford Rivers. The name
Bedford here comes from the Dukes of Bedford who were the
main investors in The Gentlemen Adventurers behind
Vermuyden's drainage plans.

As well as the Wildfowl and Wetlands Trust, the Royal
Society for the Protection of Birds and the Wildford Trust of
Bedfordshire and Cambridgeshire also own land in the area, so
conservation is a major issue in the Fens which now provide one
of the most important concentrations of wildlife in Europe. A
wide range of animals and wild flowers can be found here, too,
offering an interest far beyond that of bird-watching.

Any effort to protect this wildlife deserves support. It is all too
frequent, and frightening, to read the story of neglect and
destruction that has taken place in this country during the last
fifty years. The populations of barn owls, lapwings, linnets and
kingfishers have been halved, as have the areas of grazing
marshes and hedgerows needed by many of our native birds.
Meadows and downland have disappeared at an even more
alarming rate. Birds and animals we once took for granted are
seriously threatened, including such favourites as the skylark,
nightingale, otter and toad. Is it really possible that the skies will
one day be empty of song because of our greed for the land
below? Already there are far fewer larks in the Fens than there
were when I was a child. Then it was not difficult to find a field
from which twenty or more larks would spring like water-jets of
song into the air, trilling away for minutes before dropping like
pebbles into the warm pool of grass in which their nests were
hidden. There are not many fields left like that now and the
skylarks have been pushed more and more into the narrow
verges alongside noisy roads. You can't expect larks to build in
concrete or tarmacadam. So maybe it's true that tomorrow's
children will never see a bird's nest in a bush, or hear a
celebration of larks, they may never watch a butterfly sunning
itself on a wild flower, or listen to the ghostly call of an owl in the
misty dusk. If half of our natural world has gone in our own
lifetime, what will be left for the future, unless the
policy-makers and profiteers can be persuaded to change their
minds and make room for all aspects of life? We may not go back
to Blake's 'dark, satanic mills' but we may have to rewrite his
'green and pleasant land' to read 'grey and sterile land'. This

may sound an over-pessimistic view rather than a natural concern for what is slowly happening year by year. I hope I am proved wrong.

iv

At least a day at somewhere like the Welney Wildfowl Centre can go a long way towards restoring one's optimism and remind the gloomy heart of what it should still be grateful for in nature.

Although the winter months are undoubtedly an exciting time to be there, it would be a mistake to give the impression that it is only a one-season centre. When the swans depart in March, to return to their breeding-grounds, other interests take over. From April to October there is a busy programme of events when the other birds on the washlands get their share of the attention. It is the turn then of the snipe, godwits, plovers and sandpipers, of beautiful marsh-flowers and butterflies. There are organized walks, lectures and adventure trails for children, or you can stroll through ancient Fenland on a summer's evening and enjoy a barbecue at sunset. As the light fails and the smoke scents the air you can quite easily imagine yourself to be one of the first settlers.

But, inevitably, the swans will return the following year to take over the lagoons and bring the winter visitors back again to watch this annual ritual. If the swans arrive early, as they did in 1992, the talk will be of a hard winter, with snow before Christmas. If that happens, and the waters are frozen, then another spectacle will be added to the landscape – fen-skating. This is something I shall be writing about in a later chapter so I must not let it intrude too much here. I will be content in these early pages to stay with the birds.

I used the word 'carnival' at the beginning of this chapter and did so because the crowded washland can easily remind you of such a festive occasion. There is colour, entertainment, and a great deal of showing-off among the birds. The swans predominate, of course. They are the stars of the show, preening and gliding about the lagoons like top fashion-models with a rather superior air. The mallards push about in little groups like gossiping cousins who haven't seen each other in weeks, and the chubby pochards strut around with the wigeon like happy bandsmen proud of their uniforms. I grew very attached to the pochards who are full of character and, almost, steal the show. There can be as many as 1,500 of them wintering here from central or eastern Europe. But, again, I must remember that they are only part of the whole. All pochards – like all swans – would make for a less interesting world at Welney as anywhere else.

Although visitors are asked to be quiet this does not apply to the birds who, between them, can set up a raucous noise that can be heard half a mile away, especially towards feeding-time in the afternoon. To enjoy all the drama of such a large arena it pays to have a pair of good binoculars but, if you do not possess your own, then the centre has them on hire for £1 a day.

In view of all this activity – and the centre's popularity – you may still be wondering how any peace or solitude can be found. But it can, especially if you live just a few miles away and can visit the washlands at almost any time. I have been there on weekdays when there has not been anyone else around. During the early weeks of winter there is often a haunting stillness. The fields surrounding the washlands are quiet, their crops of potatoes and sugar-beet have been lifted and sent on their way. The black land has been ploughed and, in some cases, already sown with winter wheat. The filament pylons stretch away into the distance and only the wind's harsh notes scrape through the bare thorn-bushes and reeds, breaking what would otherwise be silence. At such times even the birds seem to respect this need to be still.

To stand in one of the hides looking out over such an enormous expanse of water is to be part of a secret world that will soon cast its spell over you. Although it might be bitterly cold and you are sure you will soon be turned to ice, you cannot tear yourself away from a scene that has become mesmeric. On a bright winter's day, with the waters reflecting the sunlight, and with frost sparkling on the grass, you are close to a beauty which civilization has not yet marred, a beauty which cannot be found all that often.

Should the cold penetrate too deeply and you have to return to the world's noisier routine, you can always call at The Lamb and Flag in the village, whether you want a coffee or whisky-mac. You will find a welcoming log fire in the grate, can order something to eat from a variety of reliable bar meals, watch the local expert darts players, or listen to the regulars quietly discussing some crucial issue or telling tales which you will find hard to believe. But, if you are sceptical and think some of the stories rather tall, just look at the stuffed pike above the fireplace. It took three hours to catch, weighs 36½lbs and is nearly 4 ft. long. Yes, some remarkable and strange things have been known to happen in the Fens.

I always feel very close to the heart of fenland life when I'm at Welney. It makes no concessions to anyone. It is as it is and you know it's genuine. Walk past the village hall and stand on the muddy river-bank near The Three Tuns, or better still on the bridge itself, and you will feel the pulse of fenland history. The Old Bedford River reaches towards infinity in both directions. You are unlikely to see a longer stretch of straight water. The isolated cottages along the bank, the willow trees standing in floodwater, the scattered farms beyond, a huge sun floating its low orb towards the horizon – all part of a great scene. And then the smell, a real fenland smell of antiquity, dampness, richness and fertility.

It is when you are standing here that you can best appreciate the vision and skill of the 35-year-old Cornelius Vermuyden, who had more than the water to contend with. When his plans were announced the people of the Fens were outraged for they knew that their lives would be changed completely. Because of their fierce resistance, and the reluctance of nature to co-operate, it took longer to drain the Fens than Vermuyden had predicted. But at Welney you are looking at two of his greatest achievements – the Old and the New Bedford Rivers that were cut from Earith to Denver in the early seventeenth century – great drains over twenty miles long, excavated manually and unerringly straight all the way.

Driving away from Welney towards the village of Manea I stopped to admire another long stretch of straightness, this time a narrow road with its leaning telegraph-poles and clumps of grass in the tarmac. In the distance one lonely farmhouse made a notch on the skyline, like the sight on a gun barrel. The rest was space. Beauty? For me, yes!

2 Our World was a Place Called Common Acre

Breathes there the man with soul so dead
Who never to himself hath said –
This is my own, my native land ...

Sir Walter Scott

In farm and field through all the shire
The eye beholds the heart's desire ...

A.E. Housman

i

It was a wild day when I set out to meet Mr Jack Kerridge at Cave Farm, near Littleport. As I drove along Forty-foot from Ramsey Mereside to Chatteris, I felt the car wobble like an inexperienced acrobat on a tight-rope. Telegraph-wires were drawn back like bowstrings and rocks of grey cloud avalanched down the walls of the sky. I have known fear on this particular road before, in blizzard and fog. But this buffeting was something new. It was a contest between me and the elements. When the weight of rain became too much for my windscreen-wipers I doubted if I would ever reach my destination.

It is not easy to find your way to a remote part of the Fens and if you make one simple error in taking the wrong road you can add ten miles to your journey. Cars cannot jump rivers or race down droves meant for large-wheeled tractors. And, have you noticed how the wrong road is always longer than the right one, that there are signposts to everywhere but the one place where you want to be?

I thought I knew the area fairly well but suddenly I was in a strange land with not a familiar landmark in sight. Hope turned to panic. I have to admit that my road-map was out of date, that I had missed the bypass I should have been travelling on, and that I was now committed to old fenland roads that do not compromise with inefficient navigators. You have to pay a high price in sweat and frustration before there's any turning back. In other words, I was lost and, although the farm I was trying to reach was within spitting distance, none of the roads I tried seemed to get me there. I bounced down narrow tracks, coped with level-crossings, where I had to open and close the gates after use. I argued, momentarily, with tractors and trailers who resented my presence on their routes. Each time I got out of the car to make enquiries I was swept off my feet and made to feel as insignificant as a piece of straw.

My appointed time of 2.15 p.m. passed and became 2.45 p.m., then three o'clock and eventually quarter-past. I was about to give up when I found a signpost that gave me hope. Battered, wind-shredded, and exhausted, I finally arrived at Cave's Farm more than an hour late to find Mr Kerridge still waiting patiently for me. He looked at me with a broad smile and bright chuckling eyes. 'You didn't give up then?'

'Not quite,' I replied.

'Well, we never do, do we!' he said. 'Come on in.'

'We never do' immediately made me feel accepted and within minutes my agitation was forgotten as I became involved in a fascinating story about Jack's lifetime association with the Fens.

His family moved from Norfolk into the Isle of Ely during the agricultural depression of 1840, his father eventually marrying into a fenland farming family from March. To begin with, however, our conversation was mainly about farming conditions at the turn of the century. Although Mr Kerridge was not born until 1916 he had the wage-books of his father's time when, in 1912 for instance, an average farm-wage was 15/- a week, with extra for piece-work at harvest. I asked him if it was true that farm-labourers drank a great quantity of beer in the harvest fields. 'I never saw it,' said Jack. 'Most of the men preferred a bottle of cold tea sweetened with plenty of sugar. That was their favourite drink to quench their thirst ... better than all them cordials, or beer. Mind you, they made up for it when the day's work was over. They weren't slow in knocking back a few pints then in the pubs.' I knew that once there were many more pubs in the Fens than there are today and asked about the 'locals' in Jack's vicinity. 'In Common Acre there were once two pubs, plus a church, a shop and a school with sixty children. That was our world. Now they're all gone.' He thought for a moment and began to smile.

There used to be some high jinks in the pubs in them days, I can tell you ... My father wouldn't allow us to go into one of them because the landlady used to do a bit of a 'knees-up' on the tables on Saturday nights, showing more than she should have done. That turned the customers on all right ...

Hoping for a few more anecdotes I asked if there were many more colourful characters about then than we have today.

Oh yes! Far more than you'll find today. We're tame by comparison. There used to be a chap who claimed that he'd been in the 1898 Gold Rush at Klondyke, and another who'd been shipping horses to Australia before the First World War. Quite a few went off in search of adventure. If a chap got a girl into trouble in them days he'd often disappear for a bit of travel until the dust settled.

Knowing that most fenmen can be stubborn and bloody-minded individuals when they want to be I asked if people were more law-abiding sixty or seventy years ago or, following tradition, law-breaking. There was another wry smile from Mr Kerridge who still has a look of mischief about him:

Well, I think what you meant to say was law-*bending*, not breaking. We don't break the law in the Fens. We change it. For instance, pubs seldom closed when they should, but you didn't tell everybody. If a landlord heard that the police were about to make a visit at closing-time he would hide all his customers in the kitchen and put out the lights. When the police came to check on him he'd offer them a drink, see them off the premises, and then call all his customers back into the bar. You can't call that breaking the law ... We used to pay into a 'hand-and-slate' club in those days, which provided a fund that was to help with handouts to those members who were on the sick-list, or in a spot of bother. We paid sixpence a week and sometimes we had quite a decent balance left by Christmas, so we'd have a real booze-up. The landlord used to bring the beer into the bar in pails and the customers simply dipped their mugs into the pail every time they wanted a refill. You can drink quite a lot like that. I remember one occasion when a customer won a live duck in a raffle and he gave it some beer to drink. The duck took rather a fancy to it and asked for more, and then more, so much so that it soon got drunk and fell into the pail of beer. But that didn't stop the rest of us filling up our glasses from the same pail ... Most pubs in those days had a piano, or someone could play the concertina or mouth-organ, so a singsong was a regular event. Hawkers used to come round selling popular song-sheets for a penny each – a bit like the 'War Cry' and we'd all join in. We made our own entertainment in those days. Even at work you'd always hear somebody singing or whistling. Most men whistled then. You don't hear that any more. Too busy listening to the damn radio.

Casting my line into a slightly different current, I said, I believe there was a fair bit of rivalry between the villages then. True? Another smile, another glint in the eye, another pause.

Rivalry? It was worse than that. We daresn't go into Southery or Manea on a Saturday night looking for girls because we knew we'd get set on. They were a rough lot there ... We all were when it came to girls. Girls, sport, even skating. You never wanted anybody else to be better than you, so it was not unusual to see a few black eyes around on Monday morning.

As he had introduced the subject of skating I turned our attention to that sport which has always been popular in the Fens. You were quite a champion skater in your day, weren't you?

Well, I don't know about champion. I never became Champion of All England, which is what you were judged by. The nearest I got to that was thirteenth. But I have skated with some of the best ice-skaters in the Fens – the Horn brothers, Alan Bloom, you name 'em ... My father was a very fine skater and so taught us as children. I think I was no older than five when I first went on to the ice. We learnt to skate by hanging on to a small wooden chair, a bit like a walking-frame. Later, we learnt to skate against the clock. Speed was the essence. No fancy stuff, just speed.

There was a time, of course, when people skated for bread and meat, to help keep their families alive. You could win a shoulder of beef, a leg of mutton, or a sack of flour. But it was still speed that counted. All that's not necessary now. It's mostly just a bit of fun these days but I can remember when we had some damn good skating out on the Welney washlands. People would skate into Ely then, to do their shopping.

Jack relit his pipe and waited for the next question. Knowing that fenmen had always had a special relationship with working horses I asked if he had any thoughts on the subject.

Yes. Life was very different on the land then. If you worked with a horse you had a companion you could talk to, rather like taking a dog for a walk. I don't see much point in going for a walk without a dog. Same with horses. Some of the old horse-keepers thought more of their horses than they did of their wives. I remember one of them saying to me – 'There's no fun in patting a tractor!' And he was right. They started work at 5 a.m., had breakfast at 6 a.m., went to the fields at 7 a.m. and worked till dinner-time at about 2.30 p.m. Then they'd groom their horses, clean the brasses and stables, finishing about seven o'clock at night – a fourteen-hour day. I remember my father saying to me when I was a young man, 'never hit a horse, otherwise I'll hit you – and harder!' There was some cruelty, of course, but on the whole the horses were treated well.

From stories I had heard from my own grandfather I knew that there was some mystique about some of the potions that horse-keepers used to make sure no one else took their horses from the stable, and I asked Jack if he'd had any experience of this.

Well, that's a difficult one because most of the potions were a secret. But it's quite true. If you rub a potion round the door-frame, or on the manger, nobody else would ever get that horse away ... However, an old keeper once told me what to do. He said, rub some milk on the horse's nose and then he'll come out. And he did.

The telephone rang and Jack disappeared into another room to take the call. I looked out across the fields and realized just how many secrets and untold stories there were still out there.

ii

Some of the accounts I have been reading about life in the Fens in the nineteenth century have referred to the use of opium. This too is a subject I shall return to in more detail in a later chapter but I decided to ask Jack if he had come across it in his lifetime. 'No, not so much in my time, but it was quite common years ago for most cottage gardens to grow their own white poppies to provide them with the drug. Mothers would give it to their babies to keep them quiet while they went to work. Now, I believe, it's more likely to be whisky!'

Without having Karl Marx in mind we moved from opium to religion and the very strong feelings that had always existed in the Fens between the Church of England and the chapels. I asked Jack for his thoughts on the matter.

I suppose a lot of it goes back to the Littleport Hunger Riots in 1816 and the way the Magistrates – most of them clergymen – sent people to the gallows and transported others for life to Australia. There were faults on both sides but the judgments were harsh. I remember when the vicar called at our house my father took him by the collar and the seat of his trousers and threw him out ... Some of them were all right, of course. I remember one who went visiting his flock on bicycle and the people liked him. When he was offered a drink of whisky he would demur slightly and then give in. Once he'd had one glass he didn't know when to stop and there were times when he was given so much that he was incapable of riding his bike home. But they thought none the worse of him for that. He was always there when anybody wanted him.

Village communities were once far more insular than they are today and everybody knew every other body's business – good, or bad. But the spirit of helping each other was more generous then than now, at least I assumed so. Jack Kerridge agreed:

Well, my mother was one of the most generous women I knew, especially to her tenants. They never went without, especially at Christmas. Most families were given a good-sized chicken and 2cwt. of coal. And if they couldn't always meet the rent on time she wouldn't push them. She knew it would come in the end. People trusted each other more then – at least I think so.

Welney washlands and a willow tree

You cannot talk very long to a fenman without introducing the subject of flooding. Everyone has his own story to tell and can recall winters and springs when homes were threatened and cattle drowned. Mr Kerridge's farm has not suffered seriously for many years now, even though the Welney washlands and the Bedford rivers can give the impression that the whole of the Isle of Ely is under water. But he was able to show me accounts of the 'Great Drowned' of 1796 when the banks did burst and the surrounding Fens were put under several feet of water, causing considerable damage to property and loss of life. This constant battle with nature has, I'm sure, helped to make the fenman's stubborn character what it is, and I asked Jack if he shared this view.

> Most likely. He's cautious, that's true. Doesn't give much away. You'll never get a straight answer from a fenman, not until he's got to know you – and that could take years! You learn to be careful. If people come here asking to see me and I don't take to them, then I'll send them off to look for me in a field somewhere half a mile away. I don't like know-alls. I had a chap come here once, banging on the door. What do you want, I asked him. He said he wanted to see Mr Kerridge. I said which one? And he said, 'The old man!' So I didn't take very kindly to him and sent him off to look for me on a tractor half a mile away.

There was a brief chuckle at the end of this anecdote and I silently congratulated myself on still being there. Not that Jack Kerridge is by any means an unfriendly, stick-in-the-mud, stubborn recluse. Far from it. He is a warm, gregarious man with a fund of stories to share – if he takes to you. In his younger days he played cricket for Ely city, enjoyed a game of rugby, spent some of the war years in the RAF, has been to New Zealand a couple of times and is fully aware of what is going on in the world. He told me:

> I like travel and holidays but the best thing about any holiday is coming back to the Fens, to the place where you know you belong. When I'm away, especially if it's near mountain country, I miss the space. Do you know, on a clear day from Littleport, I can see the sun setting beyond the brickyard chimneys in Whittlesey. Where else could you see that? [As Whittlesey is my home town I warmed to him even more.] And another thing I like about the Fens is that people take a pride in their work, at least

on the land they do ... I can't abide sloppy workmanship. If a job's worth doing at all it's worth doing well. Whatever it is you should take pride in it ...

iii

I had long forgotten about my frustration and anger in getting lost. Sitting there in that quiet room I felt I had known Jack Kerridge all my life. After we had been talking for over two hours Mrs Kerridge knocked on the door and came in with a tray of tea and biscuits. The conversation turned to the seasons. Which was Jack's favourite season of the year? Without hesitation he said, 'Spring, when the earth is crumbled up and looks new and the birds are singing again ... Growth, that's what I like to see. Spring is a time of growth, hope, and light evenings. I like the days to be as long as possible...'

Having heard conflicting opinions on the future of the Fens during the past year or so I asked Jack whether he saw many serious changes taking place during the next twenty to thirty years.

> The Fens are always changing. You've got to expect that. They say that the soil out here shrinks the height of a man every hundred years. It's no longer deep enough to grow good celery, not the long white celery we used to be famous for years ago. We're all ploughing up clay now ... And, you have to remember too, that a lot of the land is no longer farmed by families like ours, families who have been at it for generations. Land here is an investment. You can never be sure what the owners are going to do next.

If the land had changed its character, what about the villages? Another relighting of the pipe and a moment to reflect, not that there was any doubt in his answer.

> They changed years ago. When machinery took over and the farm-workers left, that was the beginning of the end. Now, half the people living around here are nothing to do with the Fens. They're commuters. It's somewhere for them to sleep. They're off in the morning at seven o'clock and not back until seven at night. You'll hear as many London accents here as local ... How can there be the characters that we had around when I was a young man?

If this was so, then I put it to him that the old tradition of story-telling in the Fens was also a thing of the past. 'Maybe! Mind you, a good story was always only as good as the beer was long. You had to keep the old-timers well lubricated. They made it an art.'

Mr Jack Kerridge had not needed any lubrication, other than the cup of tea provided by his wife, and he had kept me entertained for over three hours. Mrs Kerridge must have read my thoughts. 'You needn't worry about the old Fenland character being dead,' she said. 'You've got one right in front of you.'

I had to agree and knew that it would be easy to spend the rest of my research time on this book with this one man. But, with darkness already stalking over the land, I decided that it was time to leave, just in case I got as lost on the way home as I had on the way out. Fortunately I did not and, although a gale-force wind was still raging, I drove back along Forty-foot knowing that my journey had been more than justified. I also felt reassured as I recalled Jack's last words to me as we shook hands. 'Come again, any time you like!' I promised I would, even if it had to be in a season outside the boundaries of this book. An afternoon with a man like that goes beyond 'research' and I knew that my own love of the Fens could only be enriched by meeting him at any time. I have even bought myself an up-to-date map so that whenever that day comes I shall not be late.

iv

A month passed before I was able to get over to Cave's Farm again to spend another afternoon with Mr Kerridge. This time I did not get lost and arrived ten minutes early. 'I thought you would,' he said. 'Come on in.'

We talked for a few minutes about the recent very wet weather before settling ourselves down in his front room. I then asked if he could recall some of the winters of his early childhood, especially what it would have been like then at his village school.

Well, I can certainly remember on some of those cold winter mornings our headmaster, Mr Harris, used to get us to pull all the desks and chairs into the middle of the classroom so we had plenty of room to get round the outside, then he'd sit on the desks and play his fiddle while we all danced round and round the room. He'd say, 'I'm not a violin-player, only a fiddler' and he used to play the sort of things you'd get at a barn dance. After about twenty minutes of that he'd say, 'Right! That will have warmed you up for the rest of the morning, so now we'll get on with our lessons,' and we'd put all the desks back in place. His wife used to ride one of them old 'sit-up-and-beg' bicycles and she had a piece of elastic sewn on to the hem of her long skirt which she then fastened to the pedal so that no one should see her ankle. But they were good people, with all the right values. He used to like a couple of pints of beer at lunch-time and would send some of the older boys down to the pub to get his jug filled. He said to the landlord one day, 'That's very weak beer you're sending me these days.' Well, you can imagine what was happening. The boys were having a few swigs themselves and then topping it up with water.

In some ways it was a school ahead of its time – co-educational in every sense of the word. The teachers did not believe in segregating the boys from the girls; just the opposite. The classes were arranged so that boy and girl sat side by side in rows and were all given the same lessons. 'We were even taught to sew on buttons and things like that,' said Jack, shaking his head as if he could no longer believe it.

I asked him how soon he started doing jobs about the farm.

I think I was no more than eight years old when I was sent to milk my first cow. When I said I didn't know how, I was told, 'then you'll sit on that stool until you find out'. The old cat certainly knew what to expect and sat looking up at the udder waiting for me to begin. I soon realized that if I squirted a teat in its direction it would lap up the milk and lick its face. It knew what was good for it. In those days milk was the great provider. I've carried pails of it into the house. From it we made butter and cheese, and used it in a score of different ways. It was the same with eggs. People were much more self-sufficient then. They kept pigs at the bottom of the garden. They had hens, goats, grew their own vegetables, patched their own clothes and mended their own boots…

What about drinking water? Where did that come from?

Off the roofs mostly. It was what we gathered in the water-butts from the barn roofs and the house. We had to get rid of the creepy-crawlies first, and sometimes a dead bird, but by the time it had been filtered or boiled it was perfectly fit to drink. Some people called it 'sparrow's tea' and others called it 'Adam's ale' – *and* it was free of chemicals.

And what about meat?

Well, you either had a pig killed, or bought from the butcher who used to come round in his van, or you caught what you could find. Hares were so numerous then that you could pick 'em up out of the field while you were ploughing. I knew a man who could walk past a hare in a furrow as if he'd not seen it and then suddenly fall back on it. He said to me once, 'Never look a hare or a pheasant in the eye because they can see the light in your eye and will know what you're after.' So he used to pass them by and then turn sharply to drop on 'em, and that was that. There were hundreds of hares in the Fens then. I can remember on one occasion that we killed three hundred in three nights. They were a terrible pest at the time. Destroyed acres of crops. Now, sadly, because of sprays and things they're almost extinct.

His pipe made him cough and he pulled out a colourful handkerchief from his pocket. 'My mother always maintained you could tell which part of the country a farmer came from by the embroidery on the borders of his handkerchief. Each county had a different pattern. It was like an accent.'

Once again the conversation turned to 'self-help' and the ways in which people tried to cure themselves when ill. Mr Kerridge said:

I had a man work for me who, whenever he was feeling under the weather, took a dose of gunpowder. I saw him do it any number of times. He'd put just enough to cover a sixpence, then toss it to the back of his throat, and swallow it. Some do-gooders thought that sort of thing shortened a person's life and tried to stop it. But it didn't stop him. He lived to be ninety-seven and his wife ninety-three, so there must have been something in it that did them good.

What was Christmas like for you as a boy?

A bit different from what it is today. Most of the men on the farm worked until four o'clock on Christmas Eve, then they'd come over to the house to have a glass of whisky before going home. Later we'd be sent to bed with a stocking to hang up and in the morning that would have an orange in it with a few nuts or sweets, and perhaps a tin toy. That was all we got and we didn't expect any more. The rooms were decorated with paper-chains and a bit of holly. We had the usual Christmas dinner and on Boxing Day most of the men went off to compete in ploughing-matches, to see who could draw the straightest ridge. Mind you, I think people in the country were better off than people in towns and cities. I never saw any children going barefoot. The families helped each other. If some of our tenants were ill and said they couldn't afford a doctor, my mother would say, 'You find the pence and I'll find the shillings' and the doctor would turn up. There were hard times, of course, but we forget them. Nostalgia is always better than reality.

I sat listening to this contented man who could have sold his land to an insurance company for a fortune but preferred to keep what was his. 'I said to them, what do I want all that money for? You can only sit in one chair at a time, or eat one breakfast at a time.' Then, with quiet pride, he added 'so we're still here and now I've retired my son farms the land ... then there's his boy.'

He could have been the man of whom Alexander Pope wrote:

Happy the man, whose wish and care
   A few paternal acres bound.
Content to breathe his native air
   In his own ground.

Mrs Kerridge came in with a timely tray of tea and we talked about some of the pranks her husband got up to when he was a boy. He and his friends were never short of mischief but it was 'mischief without the vandalism you get today'. Most of the tricks were played on men leaving the pub at nights, a little the worse for wear – like the one who staggered out of the bar to find that his horse had been switched round in the shafts so that when the driver climbed on to his cart he was facing the horse.

I watched the daylight fade and darkness flood in like a tide. Reluctantly it was again time to leave. When we stopped outside we saw an almost full moon rising over the fields. 'You're going to have a lovely drive home in the moonlight,' Jack Kerridge said, encouragingly. 'Mind how you go. And do come to see us again when you've got time.'

I promised to be back in the New Year and then set off in the vast, eerie stillness of a fenland night.

3 Something Brewing

St George he was for England
And before he killed the dragon,
He drank a pint of English ale
Out of an English flagon.

G.K. Chesterton

'For a pint of ale is a dish for a king ...

Shakespeare

i

As someone who has only ever been at the consuming end of the
beer industry, I was eager to accept an invitation for Mr Nigel
Elgood to visit his brewery on the North Brink at Wisbech. It
was a most absorbing experience, not unlike that of going
backstage at some major theatrical production to see how the
scenery moves. Once you have smelt the grease paint and have
witnessed what hard work the world of illusion is, you know that
your next visit to the theatre will be seen through different eyes.
Similarly, since my tour of a brewery, each pint I imbibe now is
savoured with a warmer respect for the men who produce the
contents of my glass.

In 1995 Elgood's Brewery will be celebrating its bicentenary
and today's family can look back on a business that has already
served the area for two centuries and has plans for the next.
During that time the firm has had to face many changes, not
only in the keenly competitive brewing industry but in the world
itself. The market dictates and the public's demands do not
always meet with the brewer's wishes. Public houses, too, have

changed their role in the community quite considerably in the last twenty-five years. They serve almost as much food now as drink, providing for families and coffee drinkers as well as the traditional connoisseurs of ale. Children in pubs is a controversial issue that divides customers into those who believe that it is good to accommodate everyone who wants to use the 'local', and those who lament the passing of the old established habits of seeking refuge in a cosy saloon-bar, away from children. For them the true character of the village pub has been traded in for that of a continental café, where the rattle of dominoes has given way to the rattle in the push-chair. The sanctuary of the taproom has been surrendered to the fruit-machine and rock music. The arguments will, I am sure, continue for a few more pints yet, until the very word *pint* is banished like many others from the English language, which it may well be before the century is out. In some drinks, such as draught shandy, it will disappear sooner and the poor publican will be faced with the problem of serving drinks in both imperial and metric measures, so confused is the new legislation now being formulated.

There have been other changes too which have contributed to the need for public houses to adapt to a different society. The exodus of farm-workers from the land into industry took away an established part of the village-pub trade which had been part of English rural life for hundreds of years. With the arrival of mechanization in agriculture went most of the gang-labour that once filled the fields, especially at harvest time when men often worked twelve or more hours a day and then consumed gallons of harvest beer. Tractors may well be thirsty for fuel but they do not match the thirst of a fenland farm-worker of old. Consequently, beers that used to be brewed specially for the summer have passed, like the stooks of wheat, into memory.

It was because of this interest in 'seasonal beers' that I first contacted Nigel Elgood, for I knew that his firm still produced its own speciality for the winter, called 'Winter Warmer' – a strong ale that you should respect like a beautiful woman for both can quickly go to your head, leaving you to rue in equal measures the temptation and pleasure.

I had driven over to Wisbech through a screen of torrential rain, fog, floods and muddy spray from sugar-beet lorries. The River Nene was flowing swiftly, as turgid as wet cement. Not even the elegant buildings along the North Brink could redeem the town on such a day. If this bleak prelude to winter was a reminder of what winters are like in the Fens, then I couldn't help thinking that I had chosen the wrong season for my book. But the weather is only part of a season and I was soon being warmly received by Nigel Elgood and enjoying a hot coffee in the gracious surroundings of his office, which overlooks the river. The brewery is still on the same site where it had its beginnings two hundred years ago. Before the buildings became a brewery there was an oil-mill and a granary, with nearby stables for the horses – altogether a most pleasant and historic setting.

ii

The town of Wisbech in 1795 was a different place from that of today, at least in character if not in size. Its population then was just under five thousand and the town was well known for its Georgian architecture, its literary society, musical life, scholars, philanthropists and banking families. Its busy port attracted a considerable volume of trade and, with it, came merchants from all over the world, especially from Europe. In 1825/6, for instance, the port handled 1,209 ships and a total cargo of over 70,000 tons. In former days the town had at least twelve breweries and seventy-two public houses, many of them brewing their own beers.

To take me on a guided tour of the brewery Nigel Elgood called on the services of his head brewer, Sir Henry Holder, an international expert who seasons his knowledge with witticisms and the occasional 'leg-pull'. Sir Henry, who must be the only brewing baronet in Britain, has an encyclopaedic memory for dates, temperatures, facts, quantities – and, naturally, other breweries! He also showed limitless patience as he explained to me how the beer finally reached the glass in my hand.

To begin with, I was surprised to learn that beer was being made in much the same way today as it was in Ancient Egypt 5,000 years ago. Was this a leg-pull, I wondered? No, it was fact. Egyptian beer was called 'bouza' and, said Sir Henry,

It is more than likely that the root of our word 'boozer' goes back that far. The vats, coppers, brewing-plant and ingredients were all very similar to those we use now. Brewing in this country only goes back to early monastic times and beer was not actually being produced commercially until the late medieval ages. By then, quite a lot of beer was also being made in the home. It was part of the staple diet and certainly much safer to drink than the water would have been. Its strength was unknown but my guess is that it was much stronger than anything made today – not that we couldn't make a very strong ale if we wanted to, but I doubt if today's drinkers could take it like their forefathers.

As I listened to the descriptions of each stage of beer-making I began to understand that the secret was not so much in the ingredients which are common to all beers, but in the skill of the brewer in deciding on the right temperatures, not only for heating the brew but also in the cooling of it. 'A few degrees either way,' said Sir Henry, 'can spell disaster.' He prides himself on having kept constant temperatures for every brew he has produced over many years at Wisbech. It was clear to me that a master brewer is a good cook as well as an experienced craftsman. He deserves the title *maestro* and I realized that I was privileged in having such a distinguished guide. From mashing to bottling, I was shown the secrets of his craft and soon learnt to appreciate why one beer has a flavour very different from another, even though the ingredients are the same. 'And don't forget,' said Sir Henry, 'when you taste a beer in a public house a lot will depend on how the landlord has kept it. Dirty pumps can ruin a good beer.'

At the end of my tour I was given a sample of each of the Elgood beers to try, at least the ones currently in production. As I sipped and savoured each small glass I looked at the many certificates on the wall, at all the awards the brewery had won over the years. Among them were the 'Winner of the 1986 Food from Britain Award for its low alcohol ale 'Highway' (the creation of Sir Henry); the 'Gold Medal Award of 1987', for its 'Mellow Mild'; the 'Electricity Council's Power for Efficiency & Production Award for 1989'; and the 'Silver Medal Award of 1990' for its 'Russet Ale'. The brewery has also produced its own special 'May Mild'; 'Autumn Golden'; 'Barleymead' and, of course, its 'Winter Warmer' in its efforts to meet the expectations of its many customers throughout the year. 'But,' as Nigel Elgood said, somewhat ruefully, 'you can't make a fenman drink what he doesn't want.' That may well be because fenmen share in the Elgood's family motto, *tenax propositi*, which

I have even seen men fishing on Christmas Day

means, so I am told 'firm of purpose', or, as it is more commonly translated in the family, 'bloody obstinate'.

There will, I am sure, be many more awards added to those already won for there are several plans for the future which are both imaginative and courageous. In addition to new beers there will be a brewery shop and conducted tours of the brewery, with attractions for all sectors of the public. If those visitors get as much pleasure out of it as I did then I know there will be several more chapters in the firm's history to be written. I hope so, if only to provide the Fens with its annual supply of 'Winter Warmer' to help fight the ague, rheumatism, depression, dark days and cold climate that we have to endure for three or four months of the year ... that is, if we need an excuse!

Any success, however, will not be won without competition, not only from other brewers in this country, but from overseas. More and more beers are being imported from the Continent and, with the abandoning of duty restrictions, greater amounts of alcohol are being brought back each year by holiday-makers. Wine-drinking in the home has taken the place of nipping down to the local for a pint before a meal and, quite rightly, there is much more concern now about going out for a drink because of the drink-drive laws which are reducing the number of road fatalities caused by over-indulgence. But all these factors still mean that less English beer is being consumed these days, so naturally less barley is needed for malting, smaller quantities of hops are needed for brewing, and fewer pubs are required to meet this slowly diminishing market.

Not all the threats come from the EC either. Strange 'knock-on' effects in nature can change the demand. One of the beer 'peaks' which once helped to compensate for the loss of the harvest trade, was the coarse fishing season which starts on 16 June in the Fens. Anglers from Yorkshire can drink almost as much as a thirsty land-worker and it was a common sight at the weekends to see convoys of coaches arriving from Doncaster, Sheffield, Hull, Huddersfield and Harrogate, filled with enthusiastic fishermen complete with rods, keep-nets, baskets and large green umbrellas, to line our river-banks. There, for hours in all kinds of weathers (and I have even seen men fishing on Christmas Day), they would compete for the considerable money-prizes to be won by the successful. The sport, however, depends on a good stock of the right kind of fish, which fenland waters always had. But when the zander fish was introduced into the rivers to help clean the waters it had dire consequences not foreseen at the time. The zander is omnivorous, so it devoured many of the smaller fish as well. Within a few seasons the stocks were so obviously depleted that the fishermen stopped coming. That, in turn, meant that the riverside pubs did not have so many customers wanting to quench their thirsts and talk about 'the one that got away'. No drinkers, no trade – and so on, and so on ... On the other hand, some of the local fishermen I have spoken to blame the northern angling clubs for over-fishing the rivers and depleting the stocks themselves. 'It's not all the fault of the zander, predator though he is,' said one man who specializes in catching pike.

Another reason given for the dwindling numbers of anglers along our river-banks is the decline in the mining industry itself. Miners, too, are a disappearing breed and, with each closure of a Yorkshire or a Nottinghamshire coal-pit goes another traditional part of a miner's life, from brass bands to fishing. Both pastimes can be expensive unless you are among the lucky prize-winners.

Whatever the reason, customers are harder to find now than even ten years ago and public houses can never be certain that their trade will last unless they do something to attract people from other walks of life.

But I will not spoil my memory of a visit to a brewery with a gloomy note because I do not believe that 'the end is near' – at least not yet. At the moment Elgood's own fifty public houses in the Fens, all run by tenant landlords, and the directors are determined that traditional English beers will survive, that the cosy bar will still provide the right atmosphere where tales can be told, old legends gain immortality, and new reputations be made, for an English pub is more than a place where you go simply to drink, or eat. It is a place where you expect to find the art of the story-teller still being practised, the village cricket-match still being talked about, and the important affairs of the world being put into perspective by men who are wholly single-minded in their views. I remember during the Falklands War one local customer defending Mrs Thatcher's decision to send in the troops. 'After all,' he said, 'you let them Argentinians have the Falkland Islands this week and they'll want the bloody Isle of Wight next.' Not the most sound piece of diplomacy, maybe, but where else can the ordinary man find a platform for his opinions?

iii

After my tour I was invited by Nigel Elgood and his wife, Ann, to have lunch with them and two other guests, Margaret and Peter Cave, with whom I was to spend the rest of the afternoon talking about the history of medicine in the Fens and some of the other personalities associated with Wisbech. For, during the same lifespan of Elgood's brewery, the town has also produced several famous people, either through birth or residency; among them Thomas Clarkson 1760–1846) who was a passionate campaigner for the abolition of slavery. He was a Quaker and a friend of William Wilberforce, who was himself inspired by Clarkson's vision of justice. Another name which became part of Wisbech's history was Peckover. Jonathan Peckover (1754–1833) arrived in the town in the eighteenth century when he started his grocery business and became interested in the growing profession of banking. He opened his own bank next to his shop and soon formed a partnership with the other East Anglian bankers so that, in 1782, Wisbech had its own branch of Gurney, Birkbeck, Peckover and Buxton, at 'Bank House' on the North Brink. The house is better known today as 'Peckover House' and now belongs to the National Trust. Part of its beauty is the walled garden at the back where, during the interval of a summer evening's recital in the house, it is a pleasure to walk.

Other famous names include Miss Octavia Hill, who was born in the town in 1838. Like her friend, Elizabeth Fry, Miss Hill became a hard-working reformer of living conditions for the poor and strove tirelessly to get better opportunities for working-class girls, many of whom were turning to prostitution. At the age of eighteen she became secretary to the Educational Classes for Women at the Working Men's College, Great Ormond Street. A few years later, with financial help from the Peckover family as well as advice from John Ruskin, she bought three houses in which to train girls in home management, fearlessly collecting rents in Paradise Place, one of the most notorious slums in London. With a keen business acumen to go with her human compassion, she was able to prove to her friends

– even to her critics – that it was possible to rent houses to the poor and underprivileged, and still make a profit. Her philosophy was to make 'lives noble, homes happy, and family life good', believing that if the right social and environmental conditions were provided, together with a sound education, individuals could be persuaded to improve themselves. She also saw the need to create around those houses open spaces and gardens so that in an otherwise grim, ugly, urban area, people could learn to appreciate beauty. From the portraits of her we can see that she would have been an attractive as well as an idealistic woman, passionate about life's gifts being available to all. During her life of service she inspired many young people to follow her example and, by the time of her death in 1912 at the age of seventy-four, her methods of training were not only well established in this country but were being copied in Germany, Holland, Russia and America where, in Philadelphia, the Octavia Hill Association has its headquarters. In London the Octavia Hill Housing Trust has 1,300 homes in its care. Her love of nature generally was also influential in encouraging Canon H.D. Rawnsley to create the National Trust in 1895.

As we shall see from the following chapter Wisbech has had some equally illustrious names in the world of medicine, so it has every right to feel proud of its past as well as its beer. I felt that the day had been a most profitable and enjoyable one for me. I drove home through a misty twilight that enhanced the landscape's own sense of mystery, remoteness, power and stillness. The distant horizon was again that vague area between earth and sky. Here and there little squares of light were glowing from farmhouse windows. At Guyhirn I stopped for a few moments and climbed up on to the river-bank to see what state the Nene was in now. Its turgid mood of the morning had quietened down and the chromium-coloured water reflected the last cold glimmer of the day. It was a precarious boundary for, at such a time, one gets a strange feeling of intimidation as well as exhilaration. I felt excited by the infinite space around me, with all its history and gentler associations, but was equally frightened by the awesome stage on which another drama could so easily be produced if nature took it into her head sometime during these winter months to teach us a further lesson in humility.

It may not have been the ideal day on which to introduce a stranger to the Fens but it had satisfied me bountifully.

4 Take One Fried Mouse and Some Opium

In these our winter days
Death's iron tongue is glib,
Numbing with fear all flesh upon
A fiery-hearted globe ...

C. Day-Lewis

We all labour against our own cures;
For death is the cure of all diseases.

T.E. Browne

i

There was a time, especially before the Fens were drained, when this part of the country was considered to be the unhealthiest place in England. The history of illness and its cures in the area makes compulsive reading. It is, in turn, macabre, comic, sad, astonishing and praiseworthy. Much of the illness was caused by the climatic and insanitary conditions which then prevailed for, as Miller and Skertchley remind us in *Fenland Past & Present*:

> There were large collections of fresh water in this Fen country – the lands being frequently flooded, the ground lay sodden for a long period. Great tracts were covered with decomposing vegetable and animal matter, so that the air was not only charged with watery vapours but by gaseous exhalations also; and these would be the cause of malaria ...

Malaria, cholera, ague and acute rheumatism are common complaints in the story of illnesses during the eighteenth and nineteenth centuries. As early as 1675 Dugdale records in his diary that, 'The ague is rife there and few strangers escape without a seasoning.' Dr Browne of Boston, writing in 1810, said, 'Many are fearful of entering the Fens of Cambridgeshire lest the Marsh Miasma should shorten their lives.' The word malaria means 'bad air' and was thought to be caused by the noxious gases given off by the marshes as they dried out in summer. It reached epidemic proportions in 1779, 1783, 1803, 1826 and 1857. H.C. Darby, writing in *Drainage of the Fens* (1940) quotes an anonymous poem about the land,

> The moory soil, the watery atmosphere
> With damp unhealthy moisture chills the air.
> Thick, stinking fogs and noxious vapours fall;
> Agues and coughs are epidemical.
> Hence every face presented to our view
> Looks of a pallid or a sallow hue ...

The 'stinging gnats and other troublesome flies' which bred in their billions on these marshes meant that people were often forced to wear silk nets over their heads to protect them from being too badly bitten. An infection could lie dormant for several months so the afflicted were liable to suffer as much in the spring as in the autumn from bites received earlier. In some of the more remote areas, where medical help was not available, patients had to find their own cures. These usually meant overdoses of quinine, opium and alcohol, with sometimes a mixture of all three if the patient felt desperate. It was a treatment that simply made most people insensitive to the symptoms rather than effecting a cure. Violent shivering or shaking announced the onset of the illness, followed by a fever and then bouts of sweating. This frequently led to a sudden death if no medical attention could be found, or, more likely, afforded. Mosquitos also became 'attached' to a house and could prolong the illness through an entire family over many months. It is still not uncommon to hear people today refer to the beginning of 'flu' as a 'touch of the shivers'.

Poor drainage and inadequate sanitary arrangements lasted well into the twentieth century, continuing to cause great misery in towns and villages. L.P. Hartley, who was born in Whittlesey in 1895, describes in his autobiographical novel *The Brickfield*, why his family moved in 1900 to the neighbouring city of Peterborough, 'The place was an open drain and responsible for my father's sore throats. I think the sanitary arrangements at Fosdyke [Whittlesey] were rudimentary. The refuse one saw in the streets – in the gutters, I mean, and even on the pavements! You could see diphtheria rising from them in a mist.'

To know more about the history of medicine in the Fens I needed to talk to a GP who'd had first-hand experience, especially in looking after patients during the winter months when depression and hypothermia can be as common as bronchitis or 'flu'. So I turned to my friend Dr Peter Cave of Wisbech, who had practised in the Fens for nearly forty years until his retirement in 1990. Much of what appears in this chapter is due to his research and enthusiastic response to my questions.

ii

There were, as we have already seen, several reasons why the Fens were considered 'an undesirable place in which to live'. But, because the problems were so severe, the history of medical progress in the district – especially since the end of the Second World War – has been impressive. Long gone are those days when patients walked into the dimly lit surgeries and demanded 'a bottle of medicine' for their rheumatics, or nerves. Gone, too, are the days when doctors were paid in kind, if at all. A brace of pheasants or plump chicken could sometimes be quite acceptable but, if every patient decided on the same kind of payment, the larder was soon overstocked with fowl. What made the settlement even more embarrassing was the fact that some of the birds had probably been stolen before being given to the doctor.

Fen people were also often reluctant to let a doctor help. Home cures were handed down from generation to generation and were considered to be perfectly safe for man, woman and child. One of the most popular remedies was opium and opium addiction was a very serious problem in the nineteenth century. Most cottage gardens had their patch of white poppies from which would be brewed a pot of poppy-head tea. Sometimes the drug would be taken in tablet form, or smoked instead of tobacco. It was used to cure headaches, rheumatism and neuralgia. It was even given to infants cutting their teeth. Farm-labourers took bottles of it to work to drink during their dockey breaks. Such indiscriminate use caused untold harm and, as Dr Charles Lucas said in his book *A Fenman's World*: 'I do think that this was the cause of the feeble-minded, idiotic people one frequently met with in the Fens.'

A reporter from the *Morning Chronicle*, investigating the abuse of opium in the nineteenth century was amazed to find that the sale of laudanum and other drugs was as common as the sale of butter and cheese. Market stalls in Ely openly displayed opium pills for sale at three for a penny, and Charles Kingsley was also able to describe in his novel *Alton Locke* (1851), how easily available the drugs were in Cambridge: 'You go into the druggist shop on market day and you will see the little boxes – dozens and dozens of them – already on the counter. Never a Fenman's wife goes by but what she calls in for a halfpennorth of elevation to last her out the week.'

An article by Dr Kenneth Warren, 'Opium Eating in the Fens' (from *Medicine in Wisbech & the Fens: 1700–1920*), has many such examples of the casual use of opium and its addictive hold on people, even when they could not afford it. Some would spend several shillings a week, often going without food to pay for it, or have it put on credit until they could. Although malarial diseases were on the decline by the latter half of the century the 'fen ague' was still common and, because of the damp climate, most people suffered from some kind of rheumatism by the time they were fifty. Beyond that their bodies could soon become deformed and, for many, it was difficult to walk unaided by the age of sixty. Unable to afford regular visits to the doctor most of them resorted to the old remedies which they knew to be an immediate and reliable reliever of their pains. Even if they did not take opium in a neat form it was to be found in many of the medicines available at the chemists, especially in *Godfrey's Cordial*. Children were given doses of this – which was openly referred to as 'knock-out drops' – almost from the moment they were born, especially if they could not sleep and their crying kept the rest of the family awake. Sometimes, baby-sitters were left in charge of infants while the mothers went out to work. If these immature guardians wanted a quiet life they simply made sure that the baby had a dose of opium in its bottle or on its dummy. The reporter from the *Morning Chronicle* told of a man who had said to him, 'I can't live without it. We have pawned everything that we can lay our hands on to get it. There is such a craving for it that we would go to extremes.'

The misery that such a craving caused was widespread and, if opium could not be had, then alcohol would take its place. In some cases both would be used together to provide the desperately sought-for relief. Dr Warren wrote of how 'Young pregnant women used the drug to delay the onset of labour by mixing it with gin. This they considered was necessary if they were to avoid childbirth on the first of May, thought to be an inauspicious date and full of bad omens. Some older women took up to thirty grains of opium a day.' Not only did it cause permanent misery among the living, it was frequently responsible for premature deaths and great suffering among those for whom there was no reprieve. A doctor in St Ives (Huntingdonshire) told the reporter from the *Morning Chronicle*, 'It is my firm belief that hundreds of children are killed in this district by the quantities of opium which are administered to them.' The mortality rate in the Fens was then higher than anywhere else in the country and it is impossible to calculate the damage done to succeeding generations by those dangerous cures.

Although the Pharmacy Act of 1868 placed the drug on the 'Restricted List', it was still easily available on the black market and still cheaper than the required volume of alcohol needed to have the same effect.

Fenmen have always had a reputation for being heavy drinkers and, in addition to the large quantities of beers they consumed, they also liked a drop of brandy. Barrels of brandy were occasionally smuggled into the area from French ships that had mysteriously gone aground off the east coast. During the Napoleonic Wars it is said that French prisoners-of-war were sometimes helped in their attempted escapes back to France by fenmen who knew those unprotected waterways. The prisoner was handed over in exchange for a barrel of brandy, or there was no deal. The officially recorded escapes from the Norman Cross POW Camp are so few that one can't help feeling that the fenmen's supply of free brandy had to be acquired in other ways.

But as drainage improved, as living conditions began to emerge from the dark ages and fen farming became more profitable, the problem gradually decreased, so much so that, in 1873, Charles Kingsley was able to write in his *Prose Idylls*, 'Ah well! At last we shall have wheat and mutton instead; and no more typhus and ague – and, it is to be hoped, no more brandy-drinking or opium-eating. And the children will live, not die. For it was a hard place to live in the old Fens.'

Although opium-eating may have come to an end because the new laws made it illegal, drinking did not and there were those who believed that alcohol was the greater of the two evils. Sir Bernard Brodie, in 1840, maintained that 'opium could never demoralize the habits and shorten life as gin-drinking did'. From some accounts which survive, it would appear that alcohol was responsible for more violence in the home, especially at weekends, than opium had been. Home-made beers and wines were often a supplement to what was drunk at the public houses. Most families made some kind of wine from plums, parsnips, carrots and marrows, and some of it was very potent. It still is. With the other social problems of the Victorian Age aggravated by liquor it is not surprising that many of the reformers and religious leaders condemned drink as man's worst enemy.

Not all cures were as dramatic, disastrous or evil as those already mentioned. Many fenmen believed that mole-skin or eel-skin garters were most successful in relieving rheumatic pains, whilst others thought that a potato carried in the pocket worked just as well. It was also common among people with chesty coughs to plaster a sheet of brown paper with a mustard poultice, which was then wrapped on to their bodies. Children especially, were made to wear a small bag of camphor under their vests to protect them from a cold and never a Saturday night passed without a weekly tablespoonful of syrup of figs and castor oil – as I well remember. These home-made administrations were mild compared with some. Fried or baked mice were once considered to be the best cure for whooping cough, together with a walk round the gasworks, or a teaspoonful of whisky in a cup of herb tea. But of all the 'old wives' cures that I saw in my childhood, I think the ones that intrigued me most were the ones for disposing of warts. These included rubbing the wart with raw meat, which was then buried in the garden. As the meat decayed so did the wart. Another method was to rub the wart with the inside of a broad-bean pod and wait for the pod to rot. There were those people who believed that you could sell your wart to someone else in the family – if they were prepared to buy it. A piece of thread tied tightly round the base of a wart would similarly ensure that, in time, it would wither and drop off, taking all your fears with it. Honeycombs were also used for healing skin complaints and I have heard of fenmen who claimed to know about the healing properties to be found in new cow-dung, which could cure anything from baldness to tuberculosis. But the cowpat had to be fresh and preferably with a sprinkling of morning dew. Nothing short of black magic was tried for every ailment and, no doubt, the black arts themselves were often called upon too.

iii

Before the gloom finally lifts from this chapter, something must be said about the prevalence of mental illness in the Fens, a condition which, two hundred years ago, was more barbarically treated than any other physical complaint. It is virtually impossible to say how many people at any one time suffered from some kind of madness because some families kept the problem a secret, others could afford to have their relatives put into private asylums without references, and others were left to the mercy of whatever solution the County authorities decided to provide. County lunatic asylums were first proposed as early as 1808 but did not become compulsory until 1845. With the Act, the old systems of handcuffs, leg-irons, straight-jackets and daily beatings were finally discouraged and a more compassionate method of nursing patients was introduced. The Cambridgeshire County Lunatic Asylum was opened on 6 November 1856, with the admission of forty-six patients. Between 1858 and 1870 over 1,130 pauper-patients – considered to be insane – were admitted. Add to this those numbers of mentally retarded people in workhouses, or hidden away by their families, and we begin to see the enormity of the problem for our less well-informed ancestors, for whom insanity was a public disgrace.

But was all this madness due only to years of opium addiction, inbreeding and isolation? What of the landscape itself? Like others, I have long held the belief that we are emotionally and physically conditioned by the nature of the land in which we grow up, that we are, as Carl Jung maintained, an 'expression of the soil that produced us'. Is it not possible, then, that a depressed landscape can have a depressive effect on certain minds not strong enough to withstand outside influences?

A few years ago, Dr A.R.K. Mitchell, who was a Consultant Psychiatrist at Fulbourn Hospital and responsible for the Fens from 1966 to 1984, expressed his views on the important relationship between a mental condition and a geographical environment,

> What I have noticed over the years is that we have had an over representation of manic-depressive disorders, which may represent a gene pool in the community, or it may reflect a psycho-biological adaptation to living in a very different, flat and stressing environment ... There is some evidence that dull, flat landscapes tend to produce more depression than expected. The argument is a difficult one, ranging between the suggestion that to be depressed in such an environment can give one survival advantages ... that anyone with a spark of energy gets out of the environment, leaving the chronically depressed behind. Or, a further explanation could be a purely genetic one which may probably operate in the Fens – namely, a gene pool for affective disorder which is then brought to the surface by the environment and the culture.

Many of the patients who were admitted to the Cambridgeshire County Lunatic Asylum between 1858 and 1870 were diagnosed as suffering from 'Melancholia and Mania; Acute Mania; Senile Mania; Imbecility; Idiocy; Dementian and Delerium Tremens, etc.' But they were by no means all farm-workers. There were 'discharged soldiers; a publican; tailor; turf-accountant; horse-groom; hawker of coals; carpenter's wife; school-teacher and shoe-maker'. However, where the cause of insanity was unknown it often appeared to be among those people who had lived in a remote part of the Fens, deprived of human contact, and subjected day after day to the flatness and emptiness around them. We also have to remember that during the agricultural depression of the second half of the nineteenth century there was a massive depopulation of the Fens – the fittest, brightest and healthiest going off to other parts of the country, or even abroad, in search of work. Only those without initiative or courage, those who, as Dr Mitchell suggested, were prepared to put up with poverty and their lot, stayed behind to procreate. The stock was therefore impoverished and many of those who stayed were too weak to resist the influence of the environment or their social conditions. Incest, drugs, alcoholism and frequent lawlessness bred a new race of lowlander that grew to resent visitors from beyond the Fens.

For the purpose of this chapter Dr Mitchell has kindly offered some further thoughts on the subject and I am grateful to him for permitting me to quote from them,

I have looked through the most commonly used psychiatric text-books in the medical library at Addenbrookes, and I can find no reference to climatic factors in mental disorders, far less anything on landscape. But the following ideas occur to me:

1   traditionally, people from N. Europe are held to be more phlegmatic, withdrawn and morose than those of southern mediterranean lands who are held to be more histrionic and mercurial.

2   if this is true, then in the north any mood change such as depression will tend to be prolonged and sustained, whereas in the south such moods will be more dramatic and short lived.

3   meteorological effects: again, weather is held to have an effect on mood

a: sunshine day after day (mad dogs and English men etc.,) leads to listlessness and apathy – hence mañana!

b: people's spirits lift in the spring with longer days and go down again in the autumn and early winter when the nights draw in (there is a form of depression known as Seasonal Affective Disorder – SAD!)

c: effect of phases of the moon – hence *lun*atic – on madness. I often heard this in the Fens. Also in Sicily I believe going to sleep with the moon shining on your face will lead to madness. Some mental disorders are cyclical and so by sheer chance a relapse may coincide with a full moon and the link be noticed, or else a folk belief becomes a self-fulfilling prophecy.

4   I do not believe that flat landscape by itself is enough. For example, the Camargue around Arles (incidentally twinned with Wisbech) is very similar to the Fens but here there is not noticeably excess depression (Van Gogh was detained here for treatment of depression but he was an incomer from flat Flanders).

My own thought at the moment is that the crucial effect comes from the conjunction of weather, climate and landscape. Thus in the Fens we have many winter months of dark lowering skies pressing down on endless flat fields or black peat. It is the repetition of this, day after day, which may well affect temperament, producing a melancholy frame of mind. Frozen dykes and meres, with the opportunity for speed-skating, and the summer months with their striking skyscapes, will bring a temporary amelioration to this melancholy. As well as depression, this temperament also shows characters of excessive thrift amounting to meanness, and a suspicion of strangers, both of which you have already noted in fen-folk. Finally, we have to take into account the additional effects of opium and alcohol, both of which in excess are depressants.

My hypothesis for the greater than expected prevalence of serious depression (as illness) in the Fens is thus based primarily on the existence of a gene pool, which in turn interacts with this melancholic temperament derived from weather, climate and landscape. The differential emigration out of the area of those of a less melancholic temperament and those less prone to depression, would further concentrate this interactive effect. I stress, this can only be a hypothesis because to date I have not been able to find any studies which would bring empirical figures to support my claim.

iv

Before we leave the subject of medicine in the Fens, it has to be said that some remarkable pioneers in healing have come from these parts. In Wisbech, for example, there was the Mason family, who became renowned as expert bone-setters. Then there was Dr Edward Bullmore, still remembered for his liberal use of the gentian violet; and Dr William Tubbs who was famous in the country for his use of 'mesmerism' in performing major surgery. A recently retired Wisbech doctor – Dr F.E. Lodge (who has also written articles on the history of medicine in the Fens) quotes from a report given by Dr Elliotson in 1854, in which there is the astonishing account of an operation performed by Dr Tubbs in April 1853, when he removed a woman's breast whilst she was under hypnosis. Invited witnesses marvelled at the man's skill and testified to his extraordinary powers over the human body. The patient said that she felt no pain and simply woke from her sleep when the operation was completed.

Much of what I have written about in this chapter is past history. To a large extent the cultivated Fens are very different now, so are most of the people because there has been a great intake of 'newcomers', especially people from the south, who have brought their own life styles and up-to-date attitudes with them. Few now have their experiences so deeply rooted in the soil as some of the characters I have interviewed. But I cannot believe that the spirit of the fenman will be easily obliterated. They may have their health centres and well-equipped hospitals; their illnesses may not be any worse than in other parts of the country; and they may relax more now with their videos than with their opium. Yet the old ways are not completely forgotten. During the past year I have been into homes where the traditional remedies are still used, perhaps for nostalgia's sake as much as any other, and it is a subject I find intruding into other chapters where fenland life in the past is being talked about. I have to admit that I have tasted one or two home-cures that are more palatable than many prescribed on the NHS though I remain suspicious of some of the 'secret' ingredients.

None of these remarks or anecdotes, however, can take away the enormous progress that has been made by the medical profession as the doctors in the Fens have continued their struggle against superstition and resistance to improve the medical care of the people.

Equally, it is true to say that most of those doctors have also contributed far more to the community than their medical knowledge. They have been involved in historical and literary societies, in arts and sporting activities, in the affairs of the church and local government, sitting on committees and getting things done. The Fens can now claim a high percentage of octogenarians, nonagenarians, even centenarians. When some-one comes to write the history of medicine in the Fens in the twentieth century, it will be a much more enlightened story than the one I heard from Dr Peter Cave and his colleagues. They, too, have earned their place in the chronicles of 'these mysterious lands' and deserve to be remembered for more than just writing out our prescriptions. But their profession has changed, too, and in the world of modern medicine it is unlikely that we shall get again the flamboyant, eccentric, individualistic type of GP that once played such an important role in many of our rural communities, men who are remembered as much for their extravagant behaviour as for their medical skills.

5   At Your Service

The Country Parson is exceeding exact in his life, being holy, just, prudent, temperate, bold, grave in all his ways ... Yet in these points he labours most in those things which are most apt to scandalize his parish.

George Herbert

I began a journey through the Fens, along dykes, where we were ready to have our horses sink to the belly (and) got by night, with a great deal of stir and hard riding to Parson Drove, a heathen place ...

Samuel Pepys

i

What a pity that Samuel Pepys could not have travelled with me when I visited Parson Drove to spend a very civilized afternoon with the Reverend John Seaman who, whilst aiming to be all those things listed by George Herbert, is not entirely grave in all his ways. He is a man with a great sense of fun as well. Nor was there any risk of a horse sinking to the belly that day. Although a strong wind stropped the land, the fields were dry and long rows of winter wheat already embroidered the black fields. The clear, razor-sharp light of the early winter sun still had a hint of warmth and, instead of muddy water, the dykes showed narrow strips of mercury, like barometers.

John Seaman is responsible for four parishes – Southea with Murrow, Guyhirn with Rings-End & Thorney Toll, and Parson Drove, where he lives in a spacious vicarage built in 1873. The house is not only his home but also a meeting-place for several groups in the community, including the village children who use the top-floor rooms for their 'Attic Club'.

We sat before a blazing log fire as John outlined for me a

57

typical week in his ministry. Apart from four services on Sundays he has a busy weekday programme with what he calls 'certain landmarks', such as taking the morning assembly at Parson Drove School on Monday, at Murrow School on Tuesday, Guyhirn School on Wednesday, and Leverington School on Friday. He is also a Governor of Murrow County Primary School and Guyhirn Church of England Primary School, seeing his work with the children as a key part of his ministry. Other sectors of the community who also need his services, both pastoral and practical, are the Mums & Tots, the Mothers' Union, the Murrow Sunshine club, the Parson Drove Friendship Club, the Women's Institutes and bible-study groups, as well as all the seasonal activities that go on throughout the year. His afternoons are spent visiting the people in his parishes, especially the elderly and the sick, whether they attend his churches or not.

No one in a country parish would ever think of keeping the vicar out. You're always asked in for a few minutes. I prefer to do my rounds by bicycle if the weather permits. I believe you have to be seen, have to be in a position where people can easily stop you if they want. You have to have time for them. The country parson is still considered to be the natural head of the community, even more so these days when the local policeman and schoolmaster do not always live in the village. It's the same with the clubs. I like going to see them and having a game of cards or dominoes with the old folk. You find out who needs you, what's going on ... much more than you would locked up in your study. You get to know whose birthday it is so that you can send them a card with a few kind words. I feel very strongly that you have to be at the rockface of where things are happening. You have to communicate before you can educate and I believe in letting people say what they think, however long it takes. You'll get there in the end. There's always time for the things that matter.

ii

John Seaman began his adult life as a schoolteacher in Norfolk and also became responsible, on a non-stipendiary basis, for three small parishes in the area. Eventually, with such total commitment to both jobs, the time came when he had to choose whether to stay in education or accept an invitation to take up full-time ministry in the Church. He felt that he could possibly serve education better, and more widely, in the Church than he could serve the Church as a part-time priest in a school.

When he was offered the living at Parson Drove, with its neighbouring parishes, his first reaction was, 'Oh no, not here!' But he soon realized that 'here' was where he was meant to be and quietly began to integrate into the community, 'to be of service'.

'Each parish is different,' he explained, 'with a strong sense of belonging to a place ... Some people who, for various reasons had to leave the area, still ask to come back here to be buried. There's a wonderful spirit of loyalty, something that has survived all the changes.'

Parson Drove is a small village surrounded by rich Fen farmland and is far from being the 'heathen place' it was called by Samuel Pepys. It has two parish churches, Emmanuel and St John's, and a Methodist Church – all of which at one time had good choirs. And, not so long ago, the village had a brass band that competed at Norwich Festivals, winning the Silver Cup for their section on more than one occasion.

I asked John how he got on with the fenland people.

Oh, they're an incredibly kind and generous people if you hit the right note. You just have to be seen as genuine. They hate pretentiousness. The Ministry is about meeting people and getting to know what they need from you. A country parson should bring stability to a community. People should know what he stands for and where he can be found. This vicarage is an open house. If I'm not here, my wife is. There's always someone to help if possible. One of the nicest things ever said to me was after I'd been here a few months. A man came up to me, looked me straight in the eye, and said 'We hope you'll stay a long while.' And for me, that said it all.

The afternoon light was fading over the fields and the burning logs now lit the room with a deep, warm glow. When a cup of tea was suggested I could not help but be reminded of some lines written in another parsonage by William Cowper,

> Now stir the fire and close the shutter fast,
> Let fall the curtains, wheel the sofa round
> And, while the bubbling and loud-hissing urn
> Throws up a steamy column, and the cups

That cheer but not inebriate, wait on each,
So let us welcome peaceful evening in ...

John's wife, Agnes, joined us and we continued our conversation about fenland traditions, prejudices, virtues and the village's future.

Yes, of course mistakes have been made in the past and we can go on licking our wounds, but that doesn't get you anywhere, which is why I like to spend as much time as I can with the young. We can only help to shape the future, not the past. If the village community is to survive as it should, you have to make the next generation feel part of it now. I don't mean by that that we should forget the history of our traditions. After all, we've recently had our Hallowe'en Party with apple-bobbing and pumpkin masks, and Guy Fawkes Night with refreshments here afterwards. The children love things like that. And so it will go on, with Christingle, Christmas and New Year's Eve, then Epiphany, and before you know where you are it's Easter. You have to make people aware of the pattern of the year in a way that they can enjoy it. We shall be taking groups of youngsters round the villages carol-singing and probably something of what they sing will stay with them until later in life, and they'll remember this place, and what it meant.

When pushed to name his favourite season, John settled for late autumn leading through to Advent.

I'm not sure whether harvest festivals are the end of summer or the prelude to winter. It seems to me that once they are over the days move very quickly towards Christmas. This year I conducted five harvest festivals, attended six harvest suppers and the auction of produce at The Swan, which took place after a short service in the bar, all within four weeks. It was a busy time but thoroughly enjoyable ... I think my first appearance at The Swan helped to turn the tide. Mind you, there were some functions I didn't attend because I'd not been invited and I realized afterwards that I should have been there. 'Where were you, vicar?' they asked. When I explained that I had not been asked they said, 'but you don't have to be asked, surely. You're the vicar!' So now I turn up at whatever's going on.

iii

The Church of England has produced some interesting country parsons over the years, from Parson Woodforde to the Reverend Francis Kilvert. Where did John Seaman fit into this tradition? Nearer to Kilvert, I'm sure, but he is still a man of our times, aware of the problems of modern society and of the greater challenge facing the Church today – a traditionalist, nonetheless, anxious to preserve the best of what the past has given.

Having accepted his calling to live and work in the Fens I asked him what the place now meant to him.

> I wouldn't be anywhere else. There's a glory about the Fens that I've really come to love, especially in the mornings. In the winter I like to be out on my bike by 8 a.m. and there's something very beautiful about seeing the sun rise out of the dewy earth, beautiful and wonderful. I often get ideas for my sermons while I'm out cycling. I like the space. We all need space. Space to think, to reflect, to hear echoes.

For relaxation John Seaman spends time in his large, productive garden growing vegetables as well as flowers, or sits quietly in his study reading. Occasionally he finds it necessary to seek a day's retreat away from his parishes but is soon back to take an active part again in the life of a community he loves to serve. 'There's one thing I will always say about fen people,' he says with conviction. 'When you have proved yourself you couldn't have greater loyalty or friendship from anyone.'

There was the sound of children in the hall and Agnes left us to attend to their needs. 'If our two have brought some of their friends home,' said John, 'it won't be long before we're frying a pan of chips. It's all part of our efforts at building bridges between the Church and today's young people, many of whom want to know what Christianity is about.'

I made several efforts to leave but there was always something else to talk about. I asked if I could call on him at another time, or even accompany him on one of his visits to conduct the school's morning assembly. 'You'll always be welcome. Come any time you like.'

iv

It was through John Seaman that I met the well-known Fenland character, Mr Percy Wright, who at the age of eighty-eight still rides his bike. Not the bike that made him famous but 'the one to keep me fit'. He was once known as 'The Green-Backed Monster of the Fens' and I asked him how he came to earn this unflattering title.

> Well, it all goes back to the 1930s when I was a racing cyclist and winning everything in sight. I think the Scots were the first to call me that, though originally I was known as 'The Green-Jerseyed Saxon'. That was because of the green striped jersey I wore, which my wife knitted for me. The word 'monster' came in when they found out just how determined I was to win every race I entered. They'd no idea what a tough lot we were in the Fens and had never met anyone like me before. I didn't mind being called a monster so long as I kept getting hold of 'the lolly', which was good money in them days.

Percy Wright was born at Harrold Bridge, Gorefield in 1905 and went to school at Sutton St Edmunds until he was thirteen. On leaving school he worked on a fruit farm for seven-and-sixpence a week from seven o'clock in the morning until five o'clock at night. He has lived in the village of Murrow for eighty-two years and, through his success as a racing cyclist, has become a legend. His name and his achievements still stand unbroken in the record books sixty years later.

His enthusiasm for bike-racing began at a local sports meeting at Wisbech St Mary's which had been organized as part of the peace celebrations at the end of the 1914-18 war. His success at other events in the Wisbech area meant that he was soon looking for competition further afield and it was not long before he was racing against some of the best cyclists in the country, winning the one mile grass-track British Professional Championship twice at Carmarthen Park, Wales, and the three-mile Scottish Championship at Glasgow. In 1932/3 he won more than 120 prizes and, in just two weeks, amassed over £63 in prize-money – which, he said with a smile of satisfaction, 'was a lot of money then when the average farm worker was getting thirty-bob a week'. It was with understandable pride that he showed me his many trophies and gold medals, including those for the unbroken records set up in 1934 – the Scottish Championship record of two miles in four minutes, twenty seconds; and the record for the five miles in twelve minutes, nineteen seconds.

> I could keep up a steady speed of nearly thirty miles an hour and increase that to nearly forty on the last lap. I left 'em standing. The South African champion came over one year to take me on but after the first race he went back home again. The father of one chap I beat was so upset that his son had lost that he got drunk and stayed drunk for a week.

But cycle-racing was mainly a summer interest, so what did he do in the winter?

> Well, I still kept in training and I also did a lot of shooting. The Fens in those days were teeming with game, especially plovers and partridges. The fields would be covered. I've shot hundreds. But don't you go blaming the wildfowler for the declining number of birds in the Fens. The sprays they've been using on the land for the past twenty years or more are to blame for that. They made a lot of the birds infertile. When we went shooting we were selective and controlled the number of kills.

You can't talk to a fenman for long without getting round to the subject of fishing, especially for eels.

> Cor blarmey, boy, if I'd had a pound for every eel I've caught I'd be a millionaire. I've known chaps around here catch 13 cwt. of eels in a weekend, and some of 'em were big ones too. I can remember one that weighed over 4 lb and it had quite a bulge in its middle. When they opened it up they found it had swallowed a water-rat. When I was a lad I used to catch eels with a ball of wool and some worms. I used to take an old zinc bath down to the dyke with me – you know, the sort we used to bath in years ago – and I'd lower my strands of wool with a few worms attached into the water and, within minutes, the eels had got their teeth caught in the wool and couldn't get off, so I pulled 'em out and dropped 'em into the bath. I caught hundreds like that. Then we used to crate 'em up and send the lot off to the fish-markets in London.

And winters? I asked. You must have known some bad winters in the Fens. 'Yes. The winter of 1914 was especially bad ... that was a right caution that was. It came late. February – March

Snow begins to fill the dykes

time. Snow half-way up our back door. Lasted for weeks. Then the floods. You always get floods if the winter is late. We don't see anything like the winters now that we used to get.'

When I asked Percy how he had managed to stay so fit all his life he said,

I've never worried. Never worried about anything. That's what puts half the people in the churchyard. When I couldn't get work on the land I opened a garage. I knew that the machines would eventually take over. I sold everything from wellies to paraffin, from kids' trousers to tractors. I knew everybody in the village at one time. You can't say that any more. Now the place is half full of strangers.

I mentioned another of his talents that I had heard about – his skill at jam-making. He had won prizes at that too, through his wife entering it in the Women's Institute competitions. But my remark was brushed aside and we returned to those glamorous days of cycle-racing. It was only when I was preparing to leave that he went out of the room for a few moments and returned with a pot of his home-made plum jam. 'Here, take this home with you,' he said, 'and see what it's like.'

I had one more question to ask Percy. In view of his national reputation in cycle racing had he ever wished to live somewhere else, other than the Fens? He replied,

Why should I want to do that? It's been all right here. It was training in the Fens that helped me to become the good rider I was. After all, you have to pedal every damn mile you ride here. There are no hills to take advantage of and you always seem to be pushing into a head wind. Racing in Wales or Scotland was a piece of cake after that.

As I prepared to leave he showed me another of his hobbies – picture-framing. He pointed to a row of wildlife pictures on the wall and said, 'doing that gave me a lot of pleasure'.

I left this delightful old Fenman, with his scores of trophies, medals, hobbies and memories, grateful that John Seaman had introduced him to me. I knew that it was more than his cycling records that would remain unbroken.

6 The All-seeing Eye, with a Nod and a Wink

All people have their blind side – their superstitions …
Charles Lamb

There is a superstition in avoiding superstition.
Francis Bacon

i

One of the definite pleasures of winter in which the Fens excel is the beauty to be found in newly ploughed fields, or better still, a field that is still being ploughed. There is nothing dainty or pretty about this beauty. The beauty is in the strength, weight, size and quantity of the land as well as in the sunlight reflecting on its muscular flanks. A ploughed field is like a magnificent horse – powerful and noble. You can breathe, watch its sinews twitch and its flesh glisten.

As I admired a man ploughing this morning I realized what a conflict of strength there is between the machine and the soil. The shiny ploughshares thrust themselves into the earth to subdue it, but the earth rolls over and, in the end, subdues the plough. The earth survives more than a season.

Far from being dead, inactive and ugly in the winter, the Fens offer a variety of scenes that complement each other. As well as the hefty shining furrows there are the fields that have already been harrowed, the fields that have been sown, and a few that have been left fallow – or, as I was to find out later when visiting a farm near Ely, 'set aside' by EC regulations that force some areas of land in the Fens to be unproductive. Even so, the huge squares of contrasting colours displayed around me today remind us again of just how tidy and efficient fenland farms are. The fields looked exceptionally neat, so well-kept and purposeful that I felt as proud of them as if they were all mine. More than one visitor has remarked on our good husbandry, which is in itself a thing of beauty, and it is not difficult to understand why some of the smaller farmers in Europe are envious of the scale on which we work in these islands.

It is not always such an idyllic sight. A long wet spell with miles of muddy roads might quickly dispel that romantic notion for a few days but on a good, clear day, when everything is seen at its best then the scenes provided by the Fens can be very satisfying indeed.

Knowing that I was going to be early for my morning appointment I stopped again to watch another field being ploughed. This time I was struck by the angle at which the tractor leaned on two wheels, as if approaching a sharp bend, even though its track was a long straight furrow that had not seen a curve in years. I could not help but think of the ploughman's forebears who would have walked as if one leg had not grown with the other, hobbling behind a horse pulling against the black tide, against that ancient sea of earth which still had hints of its affinity with water before the land was drained. Not much had changed. The machine still limped, working at a tilt, as if it might slide off into the dark should it not ride cautiously the laws of gravity. On such a table-top landscape it is surprising how many things do lean – farmhouses, barns, tractors, telegraph-poles, even the willow trees near the dykes look as if they might at any minute slip down some gentle precipice, leaving the earth more naked than it is. And which will win? The earth, or space? It seems sometimes as if we are held between two powerful magnets. One we can see, the other feel. The thrill of speculation comes with contemplating what would happen should either loose its pull. There are no safety barriers here.

ii

But this is not supposed to be a chapter of gloom or about ploughing. All these scenes were mere serendipitous distractions on my way from Crowland to Gorefield where I was to meet another writer, Mrs Polly Howat, a person with an enthusiastic interest in fen folklore, home-cures, ghosts, superstitions and even witches.

Pintail Cottage, Honeyhill, could easily be mistaken for a fictitious address in one of her own stories but it is real and, from her window, I was able to look out over a fen landscape that was shining under a light of such lustre that the tractors and heaps of sugar-beet looked beautiful.

Polly was born in Hampshire and lived in Somerset before settling in the Fens, so I was eager to get an outsider's view of the area and its people. I use the word 'outsider' kindly for I am aware that her knowledge and love of the Fens are deeper than that which many of the natives could claim. Her involvement in the rural life of Cambridgeshire has taken her into remote communities where several of the old traditions still survive. Her research has been systematic and she has a good nose for an interesting story.

We talked first of all about familiar customs and fenland attitudes. Polly admitted that when she arrived she was puzzled by what she saw.

It was as if the people were welded to the land and afraid of heights. There they were, under this great sky, as if it intimidated them. I was even told that the men didn't really like going up ladders. But I think I felt for the women most of all. They had such modest expectations of what life had to offer. All they knew was hard work and a very rare day out at Hunstanton – if they were lucky. Some never had a day's holiday. Another thing that struck me, and you must understand that these were first impressions, was the local accent which seemed as flat as the land. I missed the West Country lilt. But I was fortunate in that I had a job which took me out into people's homes so I had close contact with them and soon got to know them fairly well. As I was there to help them they began to trust me and it wasn't long before I felt that I was among some jolly nice poeple – straightforward, blunt, but genuine. It was through visiting them that I became converted to the Fens themselves and now I love them as much as anywhere. And the more I came to know the people the more I realized that there were some wonderful characters out there, independently minded people who knew how to enjoy themselves. They seemed to derive so much pleasure from the simple things in life – dances and socials in the village hall, parties, harvest suppers, family get-togethers and any excuse for a bit of a celebration. I was fascinated and completely won over ... so here I am.

Although Polly had always been interested in folklore it was not until she went to live in Marshland St James that she became inquisitive about fenland legends, mainly because of the village's connections with a character called Tom Hickathrift – a famous giant-killer who has appeared in various forms and is represented in fairy-stories, songs and ballads in several parts of the country. John Clare, the Helpston poet, certainly knew of his existence and recalled in his autobiographical sketches that he loved reading of Hickathrift's adventures in the sixpenny chap books that were hawked from door to door in the nineteenth century. But it is Marshland that claims this character as its son and it was here that he was supposedly born in Saxon times. He was himself something of a giant, 'being a man at ten years of age, over six feet tall and three feet wide'.

It was, however, the name of Hickathrift's friend, Henry Nonsuch, that appealed to Polly most for it was after him that her house was named. Her first question was, 'Who was Henry Nonsuch?' He was the one person to beat Tom Hickathrift in a fight and, as a result, they went into partnership as defenders of any cause they believed to be 'right and just'. They were, in some ways, an earlier version of Don Quixote and Sancho Panza and·their exploits have no doubt been subjected to similar liberties. Like all legends of such antiquity the truth can only be surmised. But the story would not have survived for so long had there not been a grain of truth in it in the first place. And when you have a grave to prove a man's existence, what more evidence do you need? As Polly Howat records in her book *Ghosts & Legends of Lincolnshire & the Fen Country*, 'Hickathrift is said to have determined his burial place by throwing a stone from his home, which landed to the east of Tilney All Saints churchyard. This is where his unmarked 8ft-long stone-slabbed grave lies at right angles with the pathway.'

But the story I most enjoyed hearing from her was the one about a character who lived much nearer to our own times and was connected with the nearby village of Parson Drove. Polly said:

Her name was Sue Wiseman, but she was also known as 'Happy

Sue' or 'Holy Hannah', though I prefer to call her 'The Woman with the Holy Hand' because she claimed that she had once touched Jesus. Ever since that day she had kept her right hand swathed in red flannel to keep in the holiness. There are still people alive today who can remember her as a 'little witchy-woman who would put a curse on anyone who displeased her' and I think she must have scared half the children to death with her funny ways and screams. It is rumoured that one night, when she was young, she met an itinerant who was dossing down in a farmer's stackyard. Their brief union resulted in a child whom she named Jesus, but she was considered to be an unfit mother so the child was taken away from her. I'm told that she kept the sorrow to herself for the rest of her life.

And if, as with Tom Hickathrift, a grave is needed as proof of a person's existence, Polly has since found out that old Sue Wiseman lies buried in a pauper's grave in Southea churchyard, Parson Drove. She died 6 November 1936. There is no stone to mark her resting-place. It was with the help of the Reverend John Seaman that Polly was able to trace the grave and leave her a few flowers.

iii

As well as hearing about all these eccentric characters, I was also eager to know what Polly had discovered about local superstitions and unusual home-cures since she had lived in the Fens.

Well, let's start with home-cures. Most of them are very similar to ones you will find in other parts of the country, with a few variations – like warts, for instance. As you've already said, there are several ways of getting rid of them. Rubbing them with the inside of a broad-bean pod was always a popular one and still is. Then there's the one with raw meat. I have actually experienced a wart being disposed of by rubbing it with a piece of meat, which is then buried in the garden. As the meat decays, so does the wart.

I had often heard my father talk about wart cures. Some people rubbed them with copper which had been soaked in vinegar, whilst some used live slugs, or herbs mixed with urine, or simply tied knots in a length of string which was then buried in the garden to rot. There were also in the Fens at one time several characters who went about as 'wart-charmers' and who, for a small fee, would work their own kind of magic to remove warts.

Superstition is never far away. Many of the objects which we now use as decorations had a much more serious purpose years ago. Horse brasses were originally worn by the horses as amulets to protect them from evil spirits or witches. Witch-bottles are still found under hearth-stones or at the backs of fireplaces in old houses which are being renovated, and people still like to hang up a horseshoe even if they have never been near a horse. Farm-horses, sadly, are such a rare sight these days that we forget all the folklore that surrounds them. It was common once for farmers to plant an elder tree near the stable door as a deterent to the 'night-mare', the name given to the hag or incubus who would ride the horse for a nocturnal adventure, leaving the poor animal all lather and exhausted by morning, so that it was not fit for work. Hag-stones were sometimes used in the stables to ward off any such evil, or even hung above the bed of the horse's owner.

Other familiar superstitions included never taking hawthorn blossom into the house because of the ill-luck it would carry, or of spilling salt which would also bring sorrow, or of putting a pair of shoes on the table, which would result in a family row. My mother was very strict about these things and became agitated if we broke any of the rules.

Polly added a few country sayings of her own. 'In my village they still say that "if the hedgerows are on the drip on Candlemas Day it will be a good year for beans" and that "a green Christmas means a full churchyard". And have you heard that "Winter thunder, poor man's death, rich man's hunger" is very often true?'

I noticed that hanging in an alcove of the room there was a bright golden ball, the size of a melon. Had there been three I would have known what it was, but only one? Was it merely a decoration or there for a purpose. It was, she told me,

a witch's ball, an all-seeing eye which deflects the evil gaze of any wicked person that looks at it. In fact the word 'witch-ball' is really a corruption of 'watch-ball' which served the same purpose, to ward off evil. Some people wonder why I want it there and I usually say because I think it is beautiful. They don't have to be golden. You can get them in various coloured glass, but they're quite hard to find. Not all witches are evil, of course. A white witch can be very kind and protective, like a guardian angel.

Some very wise and clever people have believed in witches. Sir Thomas Browne, that distinguished scholar, doctor and author of such classics as *Religio Medici, Urn Burial* and *Christian Morals,* wrote in 1643, 'For my part, I have ever believed, and do now know, that there are witches.'

And what about ghosts? Several people I have spoken to in the Fens over these past few months have assured me that they have seen a ghost at some time in their lives. I asked Mr Jack Kerridge if he had ever seen one? 'Ah! plenty in my time. But there was always an old boy under the sheet, out to scare someone. You get a lot of optical illusions in the Fens, especially in mist and near water. I've known the wind suddenly gust up a swirl of mist in the moonlight and that looked very much like a ghost.'

It is not difficult to find haunted houses in the Fens. Every village and town has them. In my own town of Whittlesey the post office was once thought to be haunted and there are reliable witnesses to prove it. So too was The Black Bull and, as Polly Howat found out, the ghost of an anxious mother concerned for her children's welfare, has been seen in a cemetery at Woodstone, near Peterborough. There was a time years ago, when people claimed they had seen the ghost of Mary, Queen of Scots, haunt the south aisle of Peterborough Cathedral where she was first buried in 1587, twenty-five years before her son, James I, moved her body to Westminster Abbey. The poet Alfred Noyes also has an episode in his poem 'The Burial of a Queen' where Timothy Scarlett, the nephew of the sexton Old Scarlett, saw the ghosts of Mary and her 'olive-skinned' lover one night as he went back to lock the cathedral doors.

Usually, when these subjects are discussed in broad daylight, they are treated light-heartedly, with a nod and a wink, for we all know that *we* are much more civilized, sophisticated, intelligent and so scientifically informed these days ever to take such supernatural things seriously. Or are we? Perhaps, occasionally, we have to agree with Francis Bacon's belief that 'there is

Reed-cutting was once a common sight

superstition in avoiding superstition' and that a broken mirror, or two spoons in a saucer, or walking under a ladder, might still invite bad luck. If so we are close then to falling within that category defined by Edmund Burke, who said that, 'Superstition is the religion of feeble minds'. And at that point we are dangerously close to another controversial issue.

I left Polly to get on with more research, more story-telling, and drove away from Pintail Cottage not really sure of what I believed. I have often been aware of 'presences' but what were they? Ghosts? Guardian angels? Witches? Figments of my imagination? Or what? I was just grateful that it was still daylight, that the large, golden-bright sun still hung, like a witch-ball, low over the western horizon and, with a little luck, I would be home before any harm could come to me. Nevertheless, I knew that I would have to go back for another talk at some time for there were many more subjects that we had not discussed – and, like a true Fen person, Polly was not playing all her cards at our first meeting. Besides, she makes very good rock buns.

iv

At our second meeting we were soon into a discussion about the Fen country and its people. Once again I enjoyed the lovely view from her window, through which the sun still shone, making the wood-burning stove unnecessary but not unwelcome, for the sweet smell of logs pervaded the house, adding to its quiet atmosphere. There, over carrot cake and coffee, we talked about women in the Fens, the part they had played and the hard lives they had endured, their struggles, resignation and achievements. It was not enough to raise large families, to keep house, to do the washing and cooking; they were also expected to help with the harvest, with pea-pulling, potato-lifting, feeding the animals, and gleaning. Polly told me,

> Some of them felt as if they had been born to work that hard, to share, serve, and to be on hand. They coped with it all with remarkable courage and good humour – wonderful people with very meagre rewards in life. The young women of today, quite rightly, would never stand for it. No wonder those older women helped themselves to a few potatoes from the fields at the end of a day's work ... They used to smuggle them out in their knicker-legs, did you know that? Just imagine. When they went to work in the mornings they looked quite slim but when they came home at nights they'd suddenly acquired these great fat thighs because their voluminous knickers were full of potatoes or swedes.

I said that they must have had very strong elastic. 'No,' said Polly, 'in those days their long bloomers would have been tied round the leg with ribbon or tape.' I had heard of 'jacket-potatoes' but this was something new.

It reminded me of a man I worked with once who came to work each morning with his small case containing no more than a packet of sandwiches and a flask of tea. But when he went home in the evening his case was full of kindling he had taken from the boss's woodshed. The firm we worked for kept his fires going for years.

Polly then talked of the many young girls who, at the age of twelve were sent into service, never to know what home-life was like again until they married and had their own children. 'And then they were back to the same old routine.'

Yes, it is easy to take a lyrical view of the past, forgetting that the simple pleasures were born stingily out of much hardship and injustice. And yet, how often had we both heard people talking about the good times they had known, of the satisfaction they had felt in belonging to a place and knowing such good neighbours. As an elderly lady in Prickwillow was to say, 'I am really pleased that I lived in that time because you knew what was what. I think a lot of people today take so much for granted. We might have been poor but we were brought up with love and always cared for. You can't ask more than that.'

Once again the clock had beaten us and it was time to leave. As if to affirm this reality of change the weather also altered course and, by mid afternoon, the strong winds of the north had hauled great nets of dark clouds into the Fens and the sky was now heavy with unborn snow.

7   The Snows and Blessings of Ninety Years

A man not old but mellow, like good wine.

Stephen Philips

A good old man, sir; he will be talking as they say, when the age is in, the wit is out.

Shakespeare

i

It is not all that often that one can share a bottle of wine with a man just a few days off his ninetieth birthday and hear him talking lucidly of winters that long ago. But Hugh Cave's memory has always impressed me, so too has the orderly way in which he has compiled his scrapbooks and journals. I have sat with him many times in his 300-year-old house in Thorney, listening to his memories of life in the Fens. I see him always as 'a man not old but mellow, like good wine'. But, on this occasion, I wanted to hear about winter and I wondered where he would begin. It did not surprise me that he started with a memory of when he was five years old.

It was in the severe winter of 1906/7 and the Wisbech Road was so blocked that the Council workmen had to dig trenches for people to cross from one side of the village to the other. Although the A47 was not as busy then as it is now it was still a main road and quite wide. I can remember my aunt carrying me across the road to the infants school beause she didn't want me to miss an attendance. I can still see the walls of snow each side of us as we struggled over. But, although several of the children managed to get there, the headmistress didn't and so we were all sent home. That was to happen on more than one occasion. I can remember, too, that when my father moved me to All Souls' School in Peterborough – which I went to each day by train from Thorney – that we sometimes failed to reach our destination because of the snow, or, if we did get through, we were often late. One March, I think it was 1916, the weather was very bad. We had walked through six inches of snow to catch the train at 8 a.m. and by 11 a.m. there was another heavy snowstorm with gale-force winds, causing serious drifting. By 2 p.m. conditions were really dreadful and I asked the headteacher if my cousin and I could leave on an earlier train to make sure of getting home. 'Nonsense,' she replied, 'what's wrong with a bit of snow?' But in the end she did allow us to catch the three o'clock train which finally pulled out of Peterborough station at 4 p.m. On the way through the town we noticed that trees and telegraph-poles had been blown down, and all the wires were strewn across the roads. It was a proper mess. We reached Thorney at five o'clock and, as it turned out, it was a good job we'd insisted on leaving early because the train we normally caught at 4 p.m. didn't make it to Thorney until seven o'clock that evening. Even then it was still one mile from the station because the line was blocked. Parents had to walk down the track to collect their chidlren and carry them home across the fields, through four and five feet of snow. But, with it being March, the sun next morning was quite warm and the snow soon melted. Then came the thaw and, of course, the fear of floods. And you don't need me to tell you what a problem they can be in the Fens. With such a rapid thaw the water couldn't get away fast enough and many farmhouses in the area were marooned. People could be cut off for days.

But, fenmen are nothing if not resourceful and I have heard of them making boats out of anything from a tin bath to a baby's pram, as well as using the usual punt or dingy. They are honour-bound not to let the elements win if they can help it. Charles Kingsley recognized this trait in them when writing *Hereward the Wake*.

> Why should the Fenman reverence Nature? He finds out soon enough … that he is stronger than Nature and right tyrannously and irreverently he lords it over her, clearing, delving, building without fear or shame. He knows no natural force greater than himself, save an occasional thunderstorm and against that, as he grows more cunning, he insures himself and his crops.

Hugh invited me to help myself to more wine and I refilled our glasses. Knowing that, among his many other public offices, he had been secretary to the Thorney Skating Association from 1928 – 1957, I asked him to tell me what he could remember of those years.

Well, my memory goes back much earlier than that, of course. I first learnt to skate in 1911 when I was nine years old. Most of us learnt on the Thorney River. We used to borrow wooden stools from the village shops to help us along until we got the hang of it. As a child I had weak ankles so they used to bandage them up to give me more support. There had to be days, if not weeks, of hard frost before you could organize anything like a proper skating-match but when we did they were great events. My father and uncle used to skate from Thorney, via the Dog-in-a-Doublet inn, on to the River Nene and from there to Peterborough, just to go to church. They must have looked quite a sight because by the time they got there they had ice on their moustaches and had to leave their skates in the porch ... I can't remember exactly which year it was but it must have been in the early part of the First World War, when we had a very hard winter, that I saw Mr Morton drive his car on to the river, which gives you some idea of how thick the ice was then. And what a treat it was in those days to go skating by moonlight! It could be very romantic, I can tell you. We had so much fun then. The trouble is, when you can look back over such a long time, you find it difficult to say what was the happiest time of your life. After all, I'm a very happy man now. I have a lot of good friends and a good family. I can't get out and about as much as I used to but I'm still alive.

The subject turned from snow to fog which, next to floods, is the worst kind of weather you can have in the Fens. The fogs usually arrive first, in early November, and no matter how well you think you know the roads you can suddenly feel as lost as a total stranger. You may as well be blind in a desert. Roads disappear, boundaries cease to exist, and the fog imposes its own chilly stillness over everything.

Hugh agreed that he would rather drive in snow than fog.

At least you can see where you're going, even if the roads are bad. For some reason we seemed to have some particularly dense fogs in the 1920s. They would descend on you without warning and stay for weeks. I remember once I was driving a lorry back from Guyhirn one day when I came face-to-face with a London-style taxi. We were both painted battleship-grey and only saw each other at the very last minute. In those days, when you slowed your vehicle down the main lights went down as well. We were both tempted to say something rude to each other but let it pass. It was no one's fault. We got by. Nowadays a bit of mist sends people into such a panic and a few inches of snow causes more chaos than several inches did then. One of the differences, of course, is that we didn't mind rolling up our sleeves and helping to clear the road. We didn't expect everything to be done for us by somebody else. I can think of one occasion, for instance, ringing up the County Surveyor to tell him that I wouldn't be able to get through that morning with my gang of men because the road was blocked. 'Nonsense,' he said, 'see the local foreman and get it cleared.' And by eleven o'clock it was. But I suppose you could say that about most of village life in those days. Everybody mucked in whatever it was. You didn't have to go on bended knee to get things done, not like you do today.

Hugh's wife, Renate, joined us and said it was time we had something to eat. 'You have been talking all morning and must be exhausted, both of you. Come and have some lunch ...'

Although the next few days were going to be busy ones for Hugh as he prepared for his ninetieth birthday celebrations, I said I would call again to see what else he had managed to find among his files and scrapbooks. I wasn't sure that he could find much more for me because I had already raided his cupboards on previous occasions for my books. But he sounded optimistic and, being a fenman, enjoys a challenge. 'Don't worry,' he said, 'you've not heard it all yet.'

ii

It was mid afternoon before I left the house and I decided to drive home along the north bank of the Nene, to make the most of what daylight was still left. I parked the car and walked on the high bank. It was very cold. In the distance the slender spire of St Mary's Church stood poised over Whittlesey like the needle of a barometer waiting for a weather change. Which way would it go? The sky was cloudless, with an icy, silvery light in the west. But behind me I could feel the deepening greyness of approaching night. Suddenly, as if the answer could not wait,

A heron waiting in the reeds

the wind stirred itself, pushing its way through the dry reeds. Nearby, a heron – which I had not noticed – was lifted like a broken umbrella and blown, all flaps and spokes, across the water to the opposite bank. The smoke from distant brickyard chimneys, which had been rising vertically a few minutes before, was now bent at right angles, drawn out like frayed wool from a spinning-wheel. When a north-easterly wind blows into the Fens it gnaws right through to the bone's marrow no matter how well you are dressed. It reminded me of a day I had spent some weeks earlier out at Welney, watching the swans coming in from Russia. The wind had the same note in its voice – plaintive, hungry and brittle. It was time to get home to a warmer temperature, to think about the snows and blessings of one man's ninety years and to contemplate, perhaps, on what memories I might retain if my own days reached that number. Hugh had set a cracking pace, as he undoubtedly would on his birthday when his family and friends joined him for his party.

iii

It says something for a man's popularity when, out of 169 invitations sent out, he receives the same number of acceptances, with many more cards from well-wishers throughout the Fens. In order to accommodate everyone it was decided to spread the festivities over two days, with two three-hour sessions each day, one in the morning and the other in the evening.

My wife and I joined Hugh on Friday morning with forty-seven other guests and it was not long before some of the conversations settled on the subject of fenland past, as well as present, comparing the times, farming, crops, winters, floods, characters and reputations. The older farmers were saying what I had heard many times in recent months: 'It's not farming any more; it's running a business. You don't need the old skills now, you leave it all to the machines ... So you should when some of 'em cost a hundred-and-fifty thousand quid. Between sandwiches and vol-au-vents memories and opinions were exchanged, interrupted and agreed with.

If you ask me we've become too sophisticated by half these days. You'll soon need a degree to cut corn! You already do! It's the

same with half these EC regulations, most of them are
codswallop ... What's wrong with our water? We're too hygienic
as it is. The body never gets chance to build up any natural
resistance to bacteria like it used to years ago. When we were
young nobody told us how much nitrate or fluoride there should
be in water ...

I heard again about 'sparrow's tea' and how the only water that
most people had then came down the gutterings from their roofs
into water-butts. 'It was a funny colour sometimes but when it
had been filtered through charcoal we drank it and it never did
us any harm. My mother always said you had to eat a peck
before you died. Ah, but what about cholera, there was plenty of
that around then, and diphtheria. You don't hear of them
anymore.' More sandwiches, more wine, more stories of snow,
droughts, harvests, the unwritten histories of earlier generations
to keep the conversations going.

Hugh introduced me to some of his other guests, including
his doctor and his priest. 'I thought I'd better have them both
handy – one for my heart, one for my soul. You never know at
my age.'

Later, when we were having a quiet chat together he said to
me again, 'Whatever you decide to write about me I do hope you
will say that I was a grateful man. It's just wonderful to see all
these people here today, it really is. I'm so pleased you were able
to come.'

Naturally the party took over and I promised Hugh that I
would call to see him on some other occasion before my book
was finished. 'I shall look forward to that,' he said, and
disappeared into the crowded room where other newly arrived
guests were waiting to greet him. It was clear to me that a person
like Hugh Cave earns friendship from what he has, in some way
or another, given to others. The years of service to a community,
the help and trust, the fun and optimistic view of life, were all
measured by the number of people who wanted to share this day
with him. It was a scene that would be repeated three more
times within forty-eight hours, leaving his family probably far
more exhausted than himself. As we left, his son said, 'He's
already talking about his hundredth and I'll be seventy then!'

You can never leave this house without having had some
laughter, some words of wisdom, and a feeling of hope for the
days ahead. As we drove away we passed the old grey abbey of

Thorney which seemed perfectly content to take second place on this special day. Even the clock had stopped chiming in his honour, as if to extend the hours beyond their natural limits, suspending time to make the most of the occasion.

iv

The days of fog that Hugh had been talking about on my first visit now became a feature of these winter months and provided a bleak contrast to the many bright days we had been enjoying. It was as Hugh had said, 'For every day of winter sun two nights of fog will follow, and it often takes another day for it to disperse.'

To wake up in the morning to find the world so transformed is a mixed blessing, especially if a car journey has to be made that day. Other car headlights suddenly gleam out of the mist like sheep eyes caught in a beam's glare when it's dark. Trees are wraith-like and buildings as ephemeral as shadows. It is not weather I like, apart from that welcome stillness it brings and, if I can spend my day at my desk, I will enjoy the feeling of seclusion and protection that is not always there when the sun is shining. Then I find it difficult to stay at home and the urge to be out in the spacious light of the Fens is one of the greatest temptations I have to overcome. I prefer writing on location, in the presence of the scene I am describing, and regret the time that has to be spent with the typewriter. But I shall not be tempted to go far today. I can stay within these walls and contemplate what it is like beyond that grey curtain at the end of the garden for I have struggled with fog often enough to know what it's like. One of the worst things about fog is its weight. It oppresses. It's like being shut in a room without air. The mind has to find a way out. Fortunately I can escape through the written word, either by reading or writing. I have to make my mind see, to project on to the page what is well-lit in the imagination. If I aim for anything definite in my work I aim to make it visual. Words have to be seen as well as heard. Images are important.

I had planned to go out to Thorney today to spend a few more hours with Hugh Cave, who has been very ill since we last met. He is worried that we shall not get his chapter finished. In a short note he sent he said, 'I hope I'm not going to let you down over your book.' I have assured him that he won't and as soon as he's stronger and the weather is better, I shall be out to see him again for I am certain that his memory gets sharper with the years.

8　And the Village Went on Talking

Winter is come in earnest and the snow
In dazzling splendour crumping underfoot
Spreads a white world ...

John Clare

What freezings I have felt, what dark days seen, What old
December's bareness everywhere.

Shakespeare

i

Some time ago I received a copy of a booklet called *Recollections of a Country Woman, 1908–1980* by Mabel Demaine, who had spent most of her life in the village of Haddenham. It was sent to me by her niece, Mrs Lorna Delanoy, who ran the Farmland Museum in the same village, and it gave a brief, unpretentious but vivid account of a childhood which, rather like Flora Thompson's, was blessed with much happiness despite all the hardships that many families experienced eighty years ago. It was a familiar story of Sunday School 'treats', street-parties, village-band concerts, chapel-outings to the seaside in summer, skating on ponds in winter, of funerals and marriages – a calendar of annual events that would not have been uncommon in most villages then. But the story was told with such affection, such sharp recall, that I wanted to know more about the author. So I phoned Lorna Delanoy and invited myself over, mainly to discuss her Aunt Mabel but also to learn something more of the history of the Farmland Museum. Both subjects proved to be engaging and I can do no better than draw first of all from the account that Mrs Demaine left for us and then to quote from Mrs Delanoy's own story of the museum. I am grateful to her and her family for so generously allowing these borrowings and warmly recommend the two publications from which they come.

A word that Mabel Demaine often used was 'treat' and, in talking to several elderly people during the past few months, I have been struck by the number of times it was used. A day out was a 'treat', so too was the harvest supper or bonfire night, or a visit to the local pantomime, or an unexpected day off school. Sometimes I learned that even my conversations with these people were looked upon as 'treats' for it gave them chance to talk about themselves and was, as one lady put it, 'better than gawping at telly all afternoon. At least you listen'. The very word meant something special, something pleasurable, memorable and rewarding – like a gift or privilege for which they were grateful. A very perky 88-year-old said to me, 'Although we often knew what was coming each year we never took anything for granted, not like today.'

Although I was familiar with such old customs as Plough Monday and May-daying, I had not heard of 'Goodening' until I read Mabel's book. It was an event that took place on 21 December each year when 'widows in ones and twos went around knocking on doors where they were then given small sums of money, or a packet of tea or sugar' which was to help out with Christmas meals. Only widows were allowed to do this but one year, a woman who was known not to be a widow (even though her husband was unable to work and was rarely seen), decided to dress in black and join the house-to-house collections. When her right to do so was challenged, she replied, 'But I'm worse 'n a widow-woman!'

What I specially liked about these memories of a fenland childhood was Mabel's love of winter stars. We had that much in common, too. Walking home from a Christmas party on a frosty night she would look up and 'watch the stars' and the important word is *watch*. If she saw a shooting-star it sent a shiver down her spine – 'It seemed such a fearful and frightening thing. I never see a shooting-star now without being reminded of those walks home on Christmas nights.' It was an experience that I had shared many times and I am certain that the fear of seeing a shooting-star was because we had been told as children that it was a sure sign of death – which, considering the number of deaths going on all the time, meant quite a few stars should be falling from our sky. I sat by my bedroom window on numerous occasions waiting for another death. If I did see a star fizzle out, leaving an emptiness where light had been, I'd shudder, wondering whose turn it was to pass on. I have since realized that if there was a death for every falling star the population would be depleted even more.

Equally appealing to me was Mabel's account of the village band out in the streets carol-playing, the bandsmen 'clustered around a lighted lamp tied to a pole' and, of course, the inevitable snow. Did it always snow at Christmas all those years ago? We like to believe that it did and certainly those are the ones we remember. As Jack Kerridge said to me earlier, 'Nostalgia is always better than reality.'

ii

Mrs Delanoy's own contribution to the literature of the Fens will, I am sure, be drawn on by future generations interested in local history for her story of *The Farmland Museum* also reveals how a labour of love can be of value to others. With help from her husband Mike, her family and friends, Lorna Delanoy ran the museum for twenty-three years, establishing a centre where every exhibit had a connection that brought history to life. I never thought I would get very enthusiastic about pieces of machinery or old tools from crafts long gone, but when you know that each item had been used by someone going about his or her daily task, without any thought of making history, then you can't help but feel a tingling satisfaction about touching the past. To walk around the garden and into the sheds was simply that, to step back into a way of life that can never return. The handle of an old plough was still warm. The iron seat of one of the earliest tractors retained the impression of where the driver had sat. Horse brasses still reflected the image of the man who had last cleaned them. Implements took on unusual shapes because of the individual way in which they had been used by the workers seventy or eighty years ago. All the weathers, aches, pains, joys and satisfactions of lost seasons were caught in a rare collection – not just of objects but of people's lives. Ploughs, cultivators, reapers, ridgers, grubbers and binders, tools once used by saddlers, coopers and basket-weavers, all part of a history that will not find much space in the nation's history books but which helped to make the Fens what they are today.

It all began inconspicuously in 1969 when Lorna's 4-year-old son, Craig, started collecting pieces of broken pottery from a recently ploughed-up garden. Among the fragments of old pots were clay-pipes, pig's teeth, and a few unidentified fossils. After washing and arranging his 'finds' in a cardboard box he announced to his family that, for a small fee, they could now visit his museum. The money he took at the door then, as well as thereafter, went to charity. During the years that followed the museum was to give £13,000 to good causes and receive more than 80,000 visitors from all over the world. The cardboard box grew into a shed, then took over the garden and the outbuildings, becoming not so much a hobby as a way of life.

As well as the usual exhibits there was a reconstruction of a labourer's cottage of the early 1920s. I stood at the door of the living-room with its peg-rugs, sideboard, table, harmonium, oil-lamp, vases, wall-clock and pictures and, among all this fine clutter, a life-size replica of the old farmhand himself, enjoying his pipe and reading a newspaper at the end of his day's work. Close by was the kitchen with its open range, cooking utensils, and a mother preparing the family's meal. There was also a child's bedroom complete with an iron cot and washstand and, next door, the wash-house with its copper, mangle, washing-dollies and blue-bag, ready for the traditional Monday morning wash-day. And, like all good museums, there was the smell of the past – hemp, wood, oil, sawdust, and a memory of the soil ploughed long before tractors and combine harvesters were invented.

This fascinating little museum has provided educational stimulus for thousands of schoolchildren who might not have had any other physical access to their history. I still find myself wanting to write about it in the present tense because the value of such a place in any area is of inestimable value. But lack of financial support and the demands of the years mean that I am now writing an elegy for it rather than trying to promote its reputation. Fortunately the Delanoys have found homes for many of the items and will retain those pieces which are of personal importance to themselves, so all is not lost. They could not have foreseen, when their young son invited them to visit his cardboard box twenty-three years ago, that his boyish enthusiasm then would have taken up so much of their time later – nor, having come this far, that it would ever end. They deserve a rest.

iii

It was through reading Mabel Demaine's book that I was also reminded of how our villages have changed in fifty years. In most of them the ponds and parish pumps have disappeared, as have many of the old pubs, shops and craftsmen. She writes, 'We had a pump just outside our back door; even in the hottest and driest summers it never failed to release for us lovely sparkling spring water. In my young days I spent hours lifting that pump handle up and down each day to supply our farm animals with water.'

When Mabel was a girl in Haddenham there were twenty pubs, a church, two chapels, the village school and a dozen or more shops. Understandably she found it difficult to adjust to modern shopping methods, with trolleys, wire baskets, everything in cans or plastic, and long queues at the check-out.

> How different it was when sugar – brown and white – was weighed up in thick blue paper sugar-bags; lard, butter and cheese cut and wrapped to order, vinegar measured into your own bottle, as was paraffin into your can. Spices, rice, cornflour, dried fruit, all the everyday groceries measured out and weighed in the shop ... slabs of toffee were broken up with a little steel mallet; elastic, lace and ribbon were measured to your required length, and the village grocer delivered the goods, his grocer-boy coming round to your door, with a long pencil tucked behind his ear.

It has been said more than once that people had more time to do things then. Time to shop at leisure, time to gossip near the bacon-slicer while waiting to be served, time to go to the shops every day if they wished. When I was a child we had a neighbour who simply walked to the corner-shop whenever she needed anything and her knowledge of what was going on in the town was extensive.

But what fascinated me most in our street's grocery shop, above all the wonderful smells and clutter, more than all the exotic aromas of ground coffee and barrels of fruit, was the speedy totting-up of the bill by the grocer. He usually wrote every item on to the blue sugar-bag and, within seconds of my mother completing her order, his pencil would skip up the columns of figures and he would write in the total. He was never wrong and quicker than any cash-register. I watched in awe, knowing it was a skill I would never acquire. Grocery shops will never be the same again and, although we are aware of the reasons why it was necessary to invent supermarkets, I think we should be grateful that people like Mabel Demaine have left us a glimpse of what life was like, both good and bad, before the world changed for all of us.

Perhaps her warm recollections owe something to her years spent living on a hill – a rarity in the Fens. From Haddenham's elevated position you are not only able to look down on the rest of the Fens but somehow you feel closer to the sun. It is easier for the spirit to rise. Some villages which are at sea-level or below, bestow their depression on the inhabitants, as Dr Mitchell suggested in chapter four. The lowest areas of the Fens can sometimes weigh heavily on the imagination, especially when the weather is gloomy. But not at Haddenham where every path and street has an incline.

As with many places in the Fens the village has gone through a variety of spellings. On a silver chalice given to the church and dated 1569, is the inscription 'for the towne of Hadnam on the Hil'. It is possible that the name originated from the Saxon 'Haeda's Homestead' and it was certainly mentioned in AD 970 as a thriving community. In the Doomsday Book it is called 'Hadreham' and when I first heard local people pronouncing the name I thought they were referring to a well-known Suffolk ale – Adnams. A former vicar of the parish, the Reverend George Fox (who served the village from 1965–1979 and became Archdeacon of Wisbech), said 'Haddenham is a microcosm of the universe' and he was not far out.

Haddenham people have always been independent and wary of new ideas until they have been proved to work. Nor are they time-wasters. 'If you have half an hour to spare,' said one villager to another, 'don't come here and spend it with those who haven't.'

I also liked the reason given for dismantling one of the two mills on the Aldreth Road – 'There just weren't enough wind to keep two mills going.'

There was a time when Haddenham had a railway. It was opened in 1866 and became known as 'The Grunty Fen Express' because the villagers said that by the time you walked down to the station it was quicker to bike to Ely if you wanted to go to market.

A house at which I remember having an excellent meal in 1972 (before giving what I am now sure was a very unsatisfactory talk on the Fens), was Porch House, built in 1657. Little did I think then that I would come to write so much about the village twenty years later, or make such good friends there. I suppose because Haddenham is on a hill I had never really seen it as a typical fenland village. In many ways this is true but I do know that the people are undoubtedly true 'fenlanders' and are very much part of the Fens' history.

iv

Then came a bonus I did not expect, or perhaps I should say 'treat', for on another visit to see Lorna Delanoy I was delighted to find myself in the company of several older residents, albeit through the wonders of the tape-recorder. Her eldest son Kevin had started recording conversations with the villagers in 1977 when he was fifteen. Lorna has a boxful of these tapes and kindly had some of them edited on to one cassette to give me 'a few winter snippets'. So now I was not only able to *read* Mabel Demaine's story of life in the Fens eighty years ago but I was able to hear her, and her friends, recollecting in their lovely accents what still remained precious in their memories.

But how do you recreate the spoken word on the page and retain its warmth, intimacy and music? I can only try to let them speak for themselves through print and hope that something of their richness comes across.

When I heard the first snippets of these tapes I was sitting in front of a log fire in the Delanoy's house, with a cup of tea and some home-made biscuits. Outside, it was a damp, miserable day that did little to convince me of the Fens' beauty, so I was happy to sit and talk, to listen and be taken back to other winters.

As some of the earlier paragraphs show I had already read about Haddenham's village band playing Christmas carols in the snow and how Mabel had walked home, stopping to watch the stars, but it meant much more to me now to hear her talking of these joys, of how she loved going to relatives at Christmas for afternoon tea, the highlight of which was the home-made ground-rice cake, far better than the ones decorated with icing and holly,

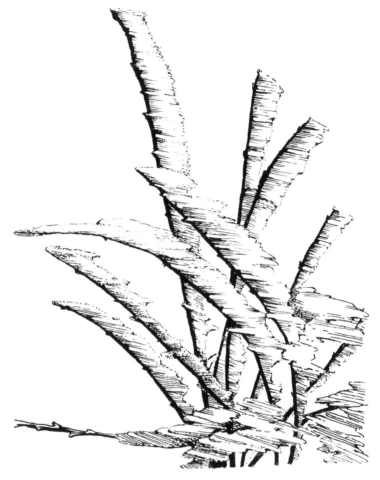

Frost sculpts its own beauty

We didn't seem to mind going out in the snow then either, but now I'd much rather stay indoors by my fire. Does the cold get colder, I wonder, as we grow older? Or do our likes and dislikes change? I can remember how we used to walk home through the snow – then, hugging our hot brick wrapped in flannel, we'd climb upstairs to bed ... such simple pleasures. One of our Christmas treats was the Sunday School tea, after which we had a magic-lantern show. The old man who came with his smoking lantern and glass slides didn't always get them in the right way up, but how we all cheered when he did ... Christmas, of course, was always a time when you realized how poor other people were, especially widows. They had no pension when their husbands died and knew acute poverty. The Parish Relief was a pittance and begging very much wounded their pride. I remember one woman who was left a widow with her invalid daughter to look after. She went out washing – you know, a washing-woman doing other people's laundry. She became bent almost double from bending over the wash-tubs, scrubbing, drying and ironing several days a week, with no washing-machines or electric irons to help. We used to see her going home, a stooping figure full of sadness …

I eavesdropped next on a conversation between George Amory and his friend Fred Wolstenholmes. George was born at Hill Row Fen in 1903 and left school when he was twelve,

> Now listen to this … I can remember when it poured with rain all night so that you couldn't get through to work next morning. You could just about walk along the edge of the water at Nor' Fen and you'd still be up to your knees in water for most of the way. Wet-footed, wet-through and thoroughly miserable. You could go nearly a mile like that. In the winter-time you wanted three 'osses to a cart to get it out of the mud. Three 'osses and that's the truth. The cart had big wheels too. They were heavy cart 'osses 'n all just to pull 15 hundredweight … We used to cart corn down to the station and bring coal back – £4 for five tons, that's what it cost.

I knew that I was going to hear more from George when we got round to the subject of the 1947 floods and I turned my attention to Charlie Ashton, the gipsy who never had a cold in his life while he slept out of doors but caught one the first time he slept under a roof,

> Many a time when I was a child I've woken up with two inches of snow on my head. But when I got married and slept in the caravan I got my first cold, at thirty-two years of age … Yes, times were hard for everybody then. I was one of thirteen children so it became a bit of a kicking match at times. The boys used to make pegs out of nut-hazel or willow and the women made flowers. My mother used to roast meat in a big old black pot – a bit of brisket or something like that. Oh the smell of that was so good I couldn't wait for it. But things were hard, weren't they? I mean, when you did get a shilling it was a shilling. Today

a pound ain't worth no more than three-and-a-tanner. Very often I used to go off with my little old dog to get a rabbit or a hedgehog ... and I'll tell you what, to kill a hedgehog you hit it on the nose and when it bleeds it's dead in no time. Then you get a stick and put him on it, then twist it over the fire to get the coat off. Then you open it up and bake 'em in clay. And I'll tell you another thing, when you taste it it's like having something that you can't get enough of 'cus that tastes so beautiful. I'd rather eat hedgehog than pig. You never know what they've been fed on.

There were memories too from Len Burton who knew some of the great skating years in the Fens, when people like Arthur Tebbutt and Don Pearson were world champions. He spoke of how people went from village to village, covering twenty miles or more in a day. There were stories too about local customs, celebrations, fruit-picking, ham-curing, butter-making, harvests, chapels and Women's Institutes – commitments to the life of a community that held it together, commitments that are disappearing with many of the old traditions as the wider and more worldly wise take over.

There were far too many hours of tape-recordings for me to attempt more than a small selection for this chapter. There is a year's work there for anyone who would like to make those authentic memories part of a local-history study, for in addition to those early recordings at Haddenham, Kevin Delanoy also recorded many more interviews at Prickwillow in 1985.

Fortunately I was able to borrow excerpts from both sets and listen to them in my own home. I was struck by the subtle differences in accents from the two villages, by their 'separateness' even though they are both within the Isle of Ely. I think I have to say that the Haddenham tapes appealed most because they were that much older and closer to the subject of this book. It was for me an added privilege to sit there listening to a village that just went on talking. Sadly, some of those story-tellers are no longer with us which is why I am grateful that the effort to record them sixteen years ago was made by a young boy who was eager to know more about the place where he knew he belonged.

9   Ploughing Within the Shadows of Antiquity

*I realized with what fresh eyes I now could see a field. It was no
longer just a bit of earth, the beauty of which I perceived from
outside ... Already I was an onlooker, a spectator, excluded as if
by excommunication from its factual and actual presence.*

John Stewart Collis

i

Anyone could have been forgiven for thinking that beyond the
distant tree-tops there was nothing – a great nothingness in
which there were no stars, no universe, not even our own
dependable sun, for it had not yet risen above the cold, naked
horizon. When it did, it was almost colourless and without
shape, neither white nor golden, but a fierce hole in the void left
by the last molten drop of creation.

This, for me, is when the space of the Fens is at its most
awesome. We know that somewhere in the great hollow the stars
still exist, that our journey round the sun will not be diverted or
curtailed, that the familiar signs will return – at least, we hope
so! But, in that exposed, abstract moment of emptiness there is a
feeling of uncertainty, a close encounter with oblivion. For we
know that if the fragile earth on which we stand also disappeared
the nothingness would be complete.

It is on days like this that we long for the reassurance of a
cloud, for the flight of a bird, or a breath of wind to confirm that
there is still some life beyond our own being. The first few
moments of any day are tenuous but when there are no familiar
signs of nature's existence it makes us even more aware of how
frail the web is, always.

I watched the sun emerging out of its 'hole' like a white-hot

disc being lifted from a furnace. For a moment it was as if I had
been struck blind. When I turned away from its unbearable light
the rest of the world was dark, a thing of the past. I opened and
closed my eyes several times before the immediate objects
around me came back into focus. Then I saw that the land was
lit by a sun that was now golden. Wet furrows glistened in its
light and the earth had already moved, like the minute-hand of a
clock, one notch further forward on its journey.

It was as if it had just come out of a coma and ached to
re-acquaint itself with all that existed – trees, hedges, fields,
birds, animals, people, buildings. In many ways it was a new
beginning. Everything on earth had been waiting for this
moment and the pure, day-breaking light was going to give us all
a second chance. A man would be a fool not to respond to the
morning's challenge.

Who, then, on such a day, can resist the call to go out into the
Fens to see the sun's light having this effect in every village and
house, on every field and farm? Early morning, especially in a
farming community, is always an important time of day. 'Make
hay while the sun shines' was never said without the benefit of
experience, nor was 'a job done by seven is worth two by eleven'.
We have taken several homespun quotations into our language
from the world of agriculture: 'doing the spade-work'; 'putting
the cart before the horse'; 'spilling the beans' and 'putting your
back into it'. And how often we hear about 'sorting the sheep
from the goats' from people who have not been near either!

ii

I had to be on the road a little earlier than usual to arrive at
Stretham, near Ely, by nine o'clock, where I had arranged to
meet Trevor Bedford, a young farmer I have known for some
time. Perhaps knowing something of my reputation for getting
lost he had suggested that I went first of all to his house, from
which he would collect me to take me to his farm near
Witchford.

Paradise Farm? Would anyone beyond the Fens ever think of
finding a paradise of any kind in this, for some, unEdenlike
country? I am the last person to suggest that this fertile corner of
England is not to be compared with man's first garden and, as
one farmer reminded me, we know 'a damn sight more about

husbandry now than Adam ever did'. So I am not surprised that someone once had the confidence and pride to call his piece of land Paradise Farm. The monks of Ely, Ramsey and Thorney were certainly not reserved in their praise of the Fens. William of Malmesbury, writing in the first half of the twelfth century said of Thorney,

> It represents a very Paradise, for that in pleasure and delight it resembles heaven itself. These marshes abound in trees, whose length without a knot doth emulate the stars. The plain there is as level as the sea, which with green grass allures the eye, and so smooth that there is nought to hinder him who runs through it. Neither is therein any waste place; for in some parts are apple trees, in other vines, which are either spread on the ground or raised on poles. A mutual strife is there between nature and art; so that what one produces not, the other supplies. What shall I say of those fair buildings, which 'tis so wonderful to see the ground among those Fens upbear?

Need I call any further witnesses? Not for the time being. There are many similar descriptions of the Fens at that time and we also know life was not always as idyllic and comfortable for many of the people who lived then. As Charles Kingsley reminds us in his *Prose Idylls*:

> Man lived hard in those days, under dark skies, in houses which we should think, from draughts and darkness, unfit for felons' cells. Hardly they lived; and easily were they pleased and thankful to God for the least gleam of sunshine, the least patch of green, after the terrible and long winters of the Middle Ages. And what ugly winters they must have been, what with snow-storm and darkness, flood and ice, ague and rheumatism; while through the long drear winter nights the whistle of the wind and the wild cries of the water-fowl were translated into the howls of witches and demons.

Paradise Farm may once have inspired a monk at Ely to write poetically but perhaps we need a little more restraint nowadays. Nevertheless, it did seem appropriate that I should now be watching a twentieth-century man ploughing a field almost within the shadows of Ely Cathedral, on land that had probably been ploughed a thousand years earlier by a labourer working for the monastery.

Trevor Bedford is now farming that land with his father and just two farm-workers – nearly nine hundred acres on the gentle side of what was once the Isle of Ely, before the Fens were drained and thousands of trees disappeared. In the strictest sense Paradise Farm is not a true fenland farm even though it comes within the Fens. Its land did not have to be reclaimed from the marshes during the periods of drainage and consequently it is heavier than fen soil. These are acres which have been cultivated since the days of Hereward the Wake and the proximity of the cathedral is a constant reminder of the 'island's' significance as well as its age. Much of the land is still Church Commissioners' land and, from some fields, it is possible to look down, as if from a hill, to the true fens below, diminishing as they are. I was reminded of some lines by A.E. Housman:

> The fields fall southward, abrupt and broken
> To the low last edge of the long lone land …

iii

Trevor's own farming pedigree is impressive. His ancestors began farming at Earith in 1640, during those years when Cornelius Vermuyden was draining the Fens. It is possible that their family surname came from the fourth Earl of Bedford who was in charge of the drainage operations which began at Earith, near the Hermitage Sluice. He would have employed local men where possible and kept an eye on the work being done. It was a day's horse-ride between the villages of Earith and Welney and the Earl is thought to have made himself comfortable in both places, fathering a few children who, later, would have taken his name and then gone on to farm his land. Trevor's ancestors farmed in the Earith area for many years. His own family moved to Stretham in 1926 and feel deeply proud of this heritage.

I had asked Trevor if I could spend a day with him, shadowing him rather than actually doing whatever jobs had to be done that day. A little wary of my ability to survive, he agreed to take me on. Having already talked with older farmers, who could remember what conditions were like sixty or seventy years ago, I now wanted to hear the views of a younger man, one faced with all the problems of farming today, producing different crops, coming to terms with the EC regulations and market controls, and trying to understand why the remote faces of bureaucracy were telling British farmers what they could, or could not, grow.

It is a subject that has many arguments for and against and I do not profess to have understood it all in one day. But I was puzzled to hear that 15 per cent of farmland that would normally have grown subsidized crops such as cereals, oil-seeds or pulses (peas or beans), now had to be 'set aside' each year and left to nature. There are very strict limits on the tonnage or acreage of certain other crops as well so British farming is not allowed to be as efficient as it can be. Land 'set aside' is simply that. It is not even allowed to be fallow. You cannot touch it, use it, or prepare it for anything. On some large farms this can mean that several hundred acres have to be left unproductive each year, which is anathema to a serious farmer who does not like to see his land growing nothing. 'For one thing,' said Trevor, 'if you're not careful the land can soon begin to look untidy.' Untidy farming in the Fens is unacceptable. Farmers, managers, foremen, land-workers, all take pride in their work and are competitive. Many years ago I knew a farm foreman who would not allow a stone to be seen on his land – not that there are many stones in fenland soil. But the land had to be clean, weed-free, and every furrow straight.

I heard from my young companion something I had heard several times, that a farmer today is more of a business manager carrying out orders. Trevor told me,

> You work for the market both at home and on the Continent, and you must grow quality – which is not a bad thing and I'm all for it. The market wants the best it can get and it's a very cut-throat business these days. Each man has to be a specialist rather than a Jack-of-all-trades. We are craftsmen now with more scientific knowledge than ever our forefathers had, or needed. Everything is calculated, whether we are growing sugar-beet, wheat, linseed or rape. You need to know about soil structure, chemicals, temperatures, markets, controls … there's no way you can call a farm-worker these days a yokel.

Trevor had already done several jobs by the time I arrived at nine o'clock and was now ready to take a 15-ton load of sugar-beet into the factory at Wissington. He told me to climb into the cab and we set off on roads that gave me the impression of bouncing across the turbulent waters of the Atlantic. Up to a thousand tons of sugar-beet are grown each year at Paradise Farm and this daily trip to the British Sugar Factory is a familiar one for the Bedfords. For me it was a complete novelty and, despite my muddy wellies and well-worn waxed jacket, I knew that I would not fool the other drivers into believing that I was anything but an imposter. The experiences that I'd had many years earlier of hay-making, pea-pulling and carrot-sorting belonged to that era before machines took over. Those labours were now too distant to have left me with any signs of being accustomed to hard manual work.

As we drove along, talking about the farms we passed, I asked about the different methods of ploughing I had seen in recent weeks, how many furrows could be ploughed at a time, how deep they could plough, and what was the comparison between the amount of work done by a modern tractor and that of the horse-drawn plough. Trevor said,

> Years ago, a man thought he'd done a good day's work with his horse if they'd ploughed an acre. Today a tractor will do anything up to twenty times that, and work in worse weather. You see, we can forget too easily just what strides have been made in one man's lifetime. It may not look as romantic now but it is far more efficient.

By now the weather was putting on an extravagant display for us. After the relatively quiet start to the day we now had very strong winds, black threatening skies, thunder, hailstorms, rainbows, and even the occasional flake of snow. The circular horizon presented a carousel of the elements in every mood that was never less than exciting.

When we arrived at the factory it was not unlike arriving at a large airport. We were channelled through certain gates, our papers were checked, the cargo weighed. Samples of the beet were taken for examination, to be checked for dirt and sugar percentage. We then took our place in the queue of other jumbo lorries taxiing into position like huge aircraft that had just landed. Lorries from Littleport, Wisbech, St Ives, Chatteris, Stow Bridge, Prickwillow and Spalding, all waiting to have their loads of sugar-beet washed and sent on their way to the refinery. I was impressed to learn that the dirty, chunky beet that had so recently been lifted out of the black soil could, within four hours of unloading, be converted into pure white sugar. The Wissington factory will receive some 3,500 loads a week totalling well over 63,000 tons of beet. It is a highly organized and efficient process. People who live in the Fens (and probably those who do not) often associate sugar-beet with muddy roads and unattractive heaps awaiting collection at farm-gates. It is not a crop that appeals like wheat or barley to the photographer but it is one that farmers like Trevor Bedford find satisfying!

> It's one of the most difficult crops we grow. For good quality beet you need not only good husbandry but the right weather conditions. As you know, we all use pelleted seed now, the beet is sown to a 'stand' – that's at certain distances – and that will determine the size of each beet. There's no such thing as singling these days. We wouldn't have the labour for that monotonous job.

When our load had finally been dispatched we made our way back through Southery, along the banks of the Great Ouse towards Littleport, Ely, and then to Paradise Farm. In some fields pockets of clay were shining in bright clods on the rest of the land.

> That gives you some idea of how much fen soil is left on some of these farms. They say that the life of a fen farm is no more than that of two men. Certainly within my lifetime 90 per cent of true fenland soil will have gone. There'll be very few root crops grown then. The soil won't be deep enough.

The thought of the Fens without sugar-beet, carrots or celery saddened me for, with the disappearance of those crops, would also go some of the smells I always associated with the Fens.

iv

As we drove back to the farm I noticed that not only were we within the shadows of Ely's antiquity but that the farm also had links with our more recent history. The concrete road on which we travelled between the fields had once been a runway for the 115 Squadron of the RAF's Lancaster and Wellington bombers during the Second World War, flown mostly by Australian air-crew, many of whom took off from English soil never to see it again. Because of its position and flatness, East Anglia became the home for thousands of airmen between 1940-45 – American and Canadian as well as Australians, New Zealanders and Britons. As I stood there in the wind and the rain, reading the details on a modest memorial column, it occurred to me that I was with a young man born after that episode in history, a man who was not only farming in the wake of Medieval England but also in the dying decade of a century that had seen more changes than any century before. And, for him, the changes that were still to come might destroy Britain's identity more thoroughly than any of our enemies had managed to achieve. But then I watched one of Trevor's men ploughing and thought of Thomas Hardy's lines, 'Yet this will go onward the same / Though Dynasties pass.'

Our next task was to check on a field of winter wheat that had been a bit erratic in its germination. I watched the skilled hands of the farmer pluck a few shoots from the waterlogged ground. He smelt them, felt them, examined them closely and said, 'I think it'll be all right. It looks a bit sick at the moment but I'll give it a few more weeks, then, if necessary, I shall have to re-drill. This has always been a difficult field.' I said it reminded me more of a First World War battlefield, adding with some haste that I was not in Flanders in 1914 but had more recently been to those war-torn areas of the Somme and Ypres. Looking at the flooded furrows on which we now stood it was hard to explain that a field this size had once been a no man's land between two opposing armies, a battle-zone on which 15,000 men could be killed in an hour. Trevor dropped the sprouting corn on the ground. 'I really haven't got much to worry about then, have I?'

Scraping the mud from our wellington boots we got back into the truck and drove away. 'I think it's time for some lunch,' he said, 'don't you?' I had to admit that my energetic morning made breakfast seem a long time ago and a bite of something would be welcome. Back at the house Trevor's wife Debbie, and their two young daughters, Emma and Katie, were waiting to hear how I had survived as a farmer's boy. The lunch that had been prepared for us was more of a banquet, with roast lamb, five vegetables, two puddings and coffee. And then it was back to work, each to his own spade.

Ploughing twenty acres a day

Having spent some time with farmers of all ages during the last two or three months I am more aware of how different the life of today's young farmer is from that of his counterpart sixty years ago – and the older men are the first to admit it. Not only is it more of a science but it is also more international and far less parochial than it used to be when farming communities kept themselves to themselves. Today, Europe is the field next door and the rivalry not always as friendly as it was with one's former neighbours. Another difference is in ownership. So much of the land now is owned by organizations not interested in farming and their business speculations have placed a false value on land they rent out. Many young men, born and bred to farm, have left the industry for other occupations with less worry. Several who stay with agriculture fail to come to terms with its demands and, as a consequence, their health suffers. Some drink heavily, others are driven to suicide. Those who survive successfully are still the true yeomen of England, the tillers of our land and the fillers of our granaries. They are proud of their husbandry and it is easy to understand why they are the envy of the world. The Fens could not be a better place for them. Even in winter the farmers' skills and achievements are there to be admired, for as Trevor Bedford said, 'You cannot easily hide your mistakes out here.'

Whatever concessions have to be made to a single market or the remote and obscure machinations that come from Brussels, a real farm is still a very personal place, a personal love, a way of life that has been handed down from father to son as a rightful inheritance. Having walked in the shadow of a young, conscientious farmer, having delivered my only load of sugar-beet, and having inspected a newly sown field of wheat, I think I know what John Stewart Collis must have felt when he wrote in his delightful book *While Following the Plough* (1946), 'I realized with what fresh eyes I now could see a field.'

10 Pages from a Christmas Diary

Heap on more wood! the wind is chill;
But let it whistle as it will,
We'll keep our Christmas merry still

Sir Walter Scott

The first Nowell, the angel did say
Was to certain poor shepherds in fields as they lay;
In fields where they lay, keeping their sheep;
In a cold winter's night that was so deep

Traditional

i

21 DECEMBER: The winter solstice. Frost on the grass, white enough to make us believe there was a light fall of snow. Blinding light of daybreak, bright enough to reach us before the rising sun came into view. Then a gull's cry as it searched for the day's first crumb, and the black filigree of branches held up like an X-ray against the light. A wonderful stillness, unspoilt by the noise of traffic that will soon dispel the dawn's calm. And soon everything was golden. The sun, burnished so brightly for its briefest stay of the year, now overawed. I could have spent another hour watching its solemn, magi-like journey across the Fens but there was the early morning cup of tea to make, the cats to feed, the dog to exercise, the ice to break on the pond, the next basket of logs to get in ready for the fire. But, once out of doors, it was a good day to be doing jobs, chatting to the postman who wished every Christmas week could be worked in such a dry, crisp light. I remember being a Christmas postman once. I had just left school and needed some extra money to spend on presents. Winter came early that year and for several days I trudged through snow and icy streets delivering the

messages of goodwill. When I left the sorting-office each morning my bag was almost too heavy to carry and one slip on the frozen pavements brought me down with a thud that no greeting of 'peace and goodwill' could appease. My curses were as blue as the bruises spreading on my body. By the end of the morning my thighs were raw, my legs aching, my fingers swollen from the snapping letter-boxes and angry dogs on the other side. And with every delivery there was always a large envelope that said PLEASE DO NOT BEND, addressed to a person who was never at home when you rang the bell, so the package had to be carried round for the rest of the day.

There was an advantage in being a Christmas postman for it gave you a good opportunity to stare into people's houses, either through their windows or open doors. You could see then how well they had decorated their Christmas trees, what kind of drinks they had bought for the festivities, and what chance there was of getting some extra remuneration. Occasionally you would be offered a mince pie or an orange and, at the end of two weeks, you might even receive a few tips which helped towards all that last-minute present-buying. But such seasonal favours did not persuade me to take up delivering mail as a profession.

This morning's postman climbed back into his heated van and the sounds of Radio One. There was no snow to upset him, no bruises waiting round the next corner. The sun was now well above the trees and shining as bright as it ought to on August Bank Holiday Monday. Only the pile of Christmas cards he'd left in my hand reminded me of what it used to be like.

22 DECEMBER: Another very sharp frost and people already beginning to look hopefully at the frozen floodwater, wondering how soon it will bear their weight so that they can put on their skates to enjoy one of the most delightful winter scenes to be found in the Fens. It won't be long if this cold spell continues and then new memories will be made to mingle with the old as winters are compared.

Less enjoyable is the ritualistic shopping that has to be done these days in busy arcades, crowded streets, and towns where the carparks are all full by 9 a.m. What should be a pleasure soon becomes wearying. The frustration, pushing, waiting, queuing and paying can dent the true spirit of Christmas. There are times when I envy those people who can get it all done months ahead of time. The young lady who served me in the bank this morning said she had bought and wrapped all her Christmas presents by the end of August. What a blissful state to be in, I thought. But I knew I couldn't do it. Harrowing though it all is in December, I prefer to cram my present-buying into these last few hectic days. The relief when it is all over is immeasurable, the excitement restored. You either have to be very wise or calculating to do your Christmas shopping in August without any signs of the Nativity scene or the piped sounds of 'Hark, the Herald Angels Sing' coming from every p.a. system.

23 DECEMBER: As I drove across the Fens today I couldn't help thinking that they would have been a good place for such an unusual birth. There are plenty of stables and, at this time of the year, most of the country roads are almost deserted. A good place for keeping a secret. In the past many a young woman has gone into hiding in the Fens to bear a child that was unwanted. Even if the local inns could have offered a room, the couples then could not often afford the luxury of a hired bed and a warm blanket – or a bribe to keep the landlord quiet. Discreet friends might help, or an empty house provide shelter. And a fenland sky would certainly have room for another star, with plenty of space for the star's journey. It would be seen for miles. Shepherds in Norfolk and Lincolnshire, in Cromer or Boston, not to mention those 'keeping watch over the flocks by night' in other lands. But which town would become our Bethlehem? Although Charles I once had grandiose plans for a summer palace at Manea perhaps this fantasy of mine is going too far. Neither Manea nor March, not even Wisbech or Ely, would be able to cope with the commercial pressures or honour should such a miracle occur on their doorsteps. Just think of all the press photographers and television camera crews!

This is not meant to be as irreverent or as cynical as it might sound. On the contrary. I just wish we could restore something of the simplicity, mystery and magic it once had before the manger and the bazaar, the sacred and the profane, became so entangled. Yet, without these pagan heirlooms we would not have the Yule-log, plum-pudding or mistletoe.

ii

24 DECEMBER: But what if, on such a night, those signs had come to a fenland sky, or that particular birth had taken place in a local barn? Would the story have changed all that much?

A SHEPHERD REMEMBERS

There was a cry in the night, neighbour.
We heard it as we sat in a field
Crouched by our fire. We thought in the dark
That a fox must have struck at one of our flock;
Life painfully torn from the belly's warmth.
But when we counted the sheep none appeared lost.
Then we heard it again and felt certain it came
From the town below. There was a death,
                But it was not a cry that we knew.

These are evil times, neighbour,
And we were afraid, imagining sounds in the air,
Thinking the stars moved and even had voices.
One, which we'd not seen before, shone over a stable.
We felt compelled by forces beyond our powers
To go and enquire. There, in the straw,
Straight from his mother's womb, lay a child,
Wrinkled and wet as a new-born lamb,
                And near his head red briars grew.

There was a light in the dark, neighbour,
We stood where the animals knelt round a manger,
Knowing there was something strange and irregular.
Having expected a death we discovered a birth.
For that we were grateful. For a moment we thought
That the child knowingly saw us, looked up and smiled.
We would have stayed longer but a cry on the hill
Sent us back to our flocks with a new hunger.
                It was nearly daybreak and a cock crew.

As always on Christmas Eve I went outside towards midnight and looked up at the sky, just in case there was something different. The wonder of expectation is as great as the wonder of hopes fulfilled. Every child knows that as it hangs up its stocking

– if children still do. Most of them these days, I believe, know what they're getting weeks before the event and there's no surprise, which is a pity.

Earlier In the evening I thought I was going to be deprived of that annual satisfaction for a thickening fog had closed in, making nearby trees invisible. But by midnight it cleared enough to leave large holes in the sky so that some stars could be seen after all. It was as if someone had broken the ice on a pond and, like a fish, I could now look up and see the world above me again. Not that our fish would have been interested. They went into hibernation weeks ago and will provide us with their own miracle when they emerge from their sleep next spring.

By the time I went back into the house it was already Christmas Day and, being a sentimentalist and a child, I couldn't resist opening some of the presents I had received.

iii

25 DECEMBER: Collected my wife's parents from their home in Leicestershire. Roads very icy with patches of freezing fog. But the hedgerows and trees were beautiful, white and weighed down with frost, as if covered in snow. Listened on the radio to Christmas Music from Venice. Monteverdi's *Exultant caeli* serene and appropriate.

A pastime which I always enjoy on Christmas Day, if there's time, is to dip into a bran-tub of other people's diaries to see how Christmas was spent in earlier times. In 1662, for instance, Samuel Pepys wrote:

> Dec 25th (Christmas Day): Had a pleasant walk to White Hall, where I intended to have received the Communion with the family, but I come a little too late ... Bishop Morley preached upon the song of the Angels 'Glory to God on high, on earth peace and good will towards men'. Methought he made but a poor sermon ... Walked home again with great pleasure and there dined by my wife's bedside, having a mess of brave plum-porridge and a roasted pullet for dinner, and I sent for a mince-pie abroad, my wife not being well to make any herself.

Parson James Woodforde's diary is another of those intimate classics, written not for fame or fortune, but for pleasure. It is a volume into which we can dip for delights at any time. Like

Samuel Pepys, John Evelyn and Francis Kilvert, James Woodforde gives a vivid account of what daily life was like in his Norfolk parish, especially during the latter half of the eighteenth century, a time when his world was changing, with the old regimes of Europe faltering and the New World of America emerging. But it was the ordinary events of his parish that Woodforde wrote about most often and, over many years, his entries for Christmas Day show a wonderful continuity of custom:

> Dec 25th, 1784: I read Prayers and administered the H. Sacrament this morning at Weston Church ... Jo Smith, my clerk, Rich'd Buck; Thos Cushing; Thos Carr; Rich'd Bates, Thos Dicker and Thos Cary, all dined at my house as usual ... I gave to each of them a shilling to carry home to their Wives before they went away ... I gave them for Dinner a Piece of Roast Beef and plumb Puddings – and after dinner half a Pint of strong beer apiece. All old Men.

A similar entry was made each year. In 1793 the Parson wrote:

> Dec 25th, Wednesday, also Christmas Day: I walked to church this morning, read prayers etc. The Singers sang the Christmas Anthem very well ... The following poor People dined at my house, or had their Dinner sent them & one shilling each ...

The following year Christmas coincided with a bad winter, with 'snow in many places quite deep, with an east wind' and not many people in church:

> The weather being so severely cold affected me so much this Morning that [it] made me faint away ... After I got home and had something warm to drink, I soon got tolerably well but could only eat some plumb Pudding & a few Potatoes. Eliz. Case, widow; Ned Howes; Thos Atterton, Snr; Chris' Dunnell, Robert Dowing and my clerk Thos Thurston, all dined at my House today & each had a Shilling. A very fine Sirloin of Beef roasted & plenty of Plumb Puddings for dinner, & strong Beer after. Took some Rhubarb going to bed.

It must have been a milder winter in 1824 for the poet John Clare, who entered in his diary on Christmas Day:

> Gatherd a handful of daiseyo in full bloom – saw a woodbine & dogrose in the woods putting out in full leaf & a primrose root full of ripe flowers – what a day this usd to be when a boy – how eager I usd to attend the church to see it stuck with evergreens (emblems of Eternity) & the cottage windows & the picture ballads on the wall all stuck wi' ivy holly box & yew ...

But I think my favourite diarist of all has to be the Reverend Francis Kilvert who, during his short ministry at Clyro created a portrait of rural life in Victorian England that has hardly been surpassed. He is at his best when writing about summer and garden parties but, for my purposes, I cannot resist his entry for 25 December 1870:

> As I lay awake praying in the early morning I thought I heard a sound of distant bells. It was an intense frost. I sat down in my bath upon a sheet of thick ice which broke in the middle into large pieces whilst sharp points and jagged edges stuck all around the sides of the tub like *cheveux de frise*, not particularly comforting to the naked thighs and loins, for the keen ice cut like broken glass. The ice stung and scorched like fire. I had to collect the floating pieces of ice and pile them on a chair before I could use the sponge and then I had to thaw the sponge in my hands for it was a mass of ice. The morning was most brilliant. Walked to the Sunday School with Gibbons and the road sparkled with millions of rainbows, the seven colours gleaming in every glittering point of hoar frost. The Church was very cold in spite of two roaring stove fires ...

But, however hard the winters were, there was in each of these writer's descriptions of winter a true ring of celebration, an awareness of what the season gave.

As we sat round our Christmas dinner table, with its lighted candles and good food, I thought of some of the amusing memories of my own childhood Christmas dinners, like the year we all ached with laughter as we sat round the table watching father trying to light the brandy for the Christmas pudding. Instead of putting a match to the brandy in the dish he tried to ignite the pudding itself which he had already baptised fairly liberally with the liquor before bringing it to the table. Failing to conjure up one splutter of flame he poured on more brandy which the pudding continued to soak up. My mother shook her head and said, 'The blessed thing will soon be stone cold if you don't serve it.' But father persisted in his frustration as our giggles added more fuel to his dilemma. And still the pudding would not light. He'll run out of matches soon, I thought, as well as brandy. Close to losing his temper he struck the next match even more vigorously, which broke in half and fell into the dish which now held a pool of the stuff and immediately a large blue flame exploded in the middle of the table. Screams joined our laughter as father now tried to extinguish the furnace he had accidentally created. When his Vesuvius at last subsided, mother said through her tears, 'Well, you'll know what to do next year!' There was no reply. The pudding was served on to our plates and, as children, our only concern then was to see if we had been given a lucky portion which contained a silver sixpence or a threepenny-bit.

None of the games we played later that day provided us with as much entertainment. It was almost as good as the year the paper decorations caught fire, bursting all the balloons and alarming our neighbours as we rushed into the garden shouting 'Fire! Fire!'

iv

26 DECEMBER: Today we found time to read some of those letters which came with the Christmas cards – those annual reports of other families' activities for the past twelve months which we did not have time to read properly when they arrived, those seven and eight pages of news which other people always seem able to write when we are struggling to add 'best wishes' to what has already been printed. One of my friends (who does not stop at eight pages) wrote from Wales, saying encouragingly,

I also have this strange passion for winter. I don't know why. Even as a child I preferred it to summer – some romantic vision, I suppose, of firelight, snow, hot toast, the smell of celery at Sunday tea-time, gas-lamps ouside, the curtains closed against the north-east winds, and *reading*! How I loved to read. It was never the same in summer, with an empty grate, with the doors wide open.

Dear to us ever the scenes of our childhood

It occurs to me now how many people share the same nostalgia, the same memories of what the winter months, and especially Christmas, meant to them, once. Even those who now claim to hate it will end up talking fondly of it in years to come. It's a 'must', if only to prove then that what *we* had was always so much better.

29 DECEMBER: White frost in the furrows and on the dyke-sides; the water in that tense stage of glistening silver before turning to ice. The sun shining clearly after days of fog. A wonderful day to be out for a winter walk. The air crisp and clean again, with slender church spires visible miles away. We were taking the dog for a walk after enjoying an excellent lunch at The Ruddy Duck, Peakirk (where every item on the extensive

menu can be trusted and each dish is worth having again). As we strolled along North Fen Road between Northborough and Glinton, I paused several times to admire the landscape. This was a walk that John Clare would have taken frequently in his search for a lost past and a lost love. He too would have known a day like this, but not our happiness. On 29 December 1841, he was taken from his Northborough home and put into care at the Northamptonshire General Lunatic Asylum, where he was to stay until his death in 1864. Although he never saw his native landscape again his memory had stored up so many images of it that even in his last years of writing he was able to recreate the scenes he had known so well.

> O dear to us ever the scenes of our childhood,
> The green spots we played in, the school where we met,
> The heavy old desk where we thought of the wild wood,
> Where we pored o'er the sums which the master had set
>
> (from *Childhood*)

And, on another occasion he wrote,

> There are spots where I played there are spots where I loved,
> There are scenes where the tales of my choice were approved
> As green as at first – and their memory will be
> The dearest of life's recollections to me
>
> (from *Stanzas*)

Nor could he ever think of his landscape without remembering the skylark,

> Wing-winowing lark with speckled breast
> Has just shot up from nightly rest
> To sing two minutes up the West
>   Then drop again ...
>
> (from *To a Lark Singing in Winter*)

The intense frost tonight must surely bring us nearer to the possibility of some skating on the Wash. That would really complete the scene.

NEW YEAR'S EVE: After a morning's work and an afternoon of music, a quiet party of three. Good food, pleasant conversation and a time to be grateful for what had been rather than make new resolutions for what might be. At midnight there was no ringing of wild bells, no sound of the old year dying or the new one being born, no voice of Robert Donat reading Tennyson's poem, as there used to be. While the logs I had cut in April now blazed comfortingly in the last fire of the year, the world outside remained eerie and silent. The minutes ticked nervously towards 'the gate of the year' and we stepped outside to see if there was anything else happening in the world. It was as quiet as the grave. Thick fog had returned and not even a cry for help would have penetrated its presence. We could not see a neighbour's house or light. We felt like the last people on earth. But the end is only a beginning. With a feeble phrase or two of *Auld Lang Syne* we went back into the house, hung up the new calendars, had a nightcap, and accepted that another year must have begun. I have always been content to live with the promise of the unpredictable in life as well as what we know to be certain – if anything is!

vi

TWELFTH NIGHT: The last day of Christmas. A time for the sweet indulgencies to be reined in as we return to normality. It is a pity that Lent doesn't start immediately after Christmas, not that I would like to lose Epiphany and the Magi, or the Service which is held each year at the tiny Chapel of Ease at Guyhirn.

I noticed this morning that there were several snowdrops out in our garden and the first green shoots of daffodils have already broken ground. What has happened to the severe winter we were threatened with when the swans arrived so early at Welney from Russia and the Arctic Circle? But it would be unwise to be complacent. As previous chapters have reminded us, some of the worst winters in living memory have come after Christmas. With nearly three months to go, spring may still be a long way off. Snow and floods have no fixed calendar. Within a season they can be very flexible. Who would want nature to be always punctual?

I was reminded yesterday that it is unlucky to keep the holly and ivy in the house after 6 January – those 'evergreen tokens of eternity' that Clare spoke of – so it must now all come down with the tree and the cards. Perhaps it is a good time too to finish the walnuts and port, to get back to a little self-discipline and work.

But not without the comfort of Sir Toby Belch's words in *Twelfth Night*, 'Dost thou think because thou art virtuous, there shall be no more cakes and ale?'

11   Mr John Thompson Remembers

The past still lives in the memory of those who have leisure to look back upon the way that they have trod, and can from it catch glimpses that may make them less forlorn.

William Hazlitt

I mean to store up a few happy memories for the long winter evenings.

P.G. Wodehouse

i

John Thompson was born at Upwell in 1855. His father came from Welney and his mother, Mary Ann South, from Outwell. You cannot claim better kinship with the Fens that that. He lived at a place called 'Susans', about three miles from Upwell Church. The house was a water-mill which the locals called 'the pepper-pot' and sixteen Thompson children were born there. As Mr Thompson admits in his story, he had very little education and could not write much himself. But he did dictate his life story to his son, John, who painstakingly wrote down in four exercise books all the things his father told him. These are now in Wisbech Museum and I shall be quoting from a typescript made of them some years ago. It consists of forty pages of single-spaced foolscap which remained faithful to the original spelling, lack of punctuation, and little regard for grammar.

Fortunately I have been given permission to quote from John Thompson's remarkable story by his own daughter, Mrs Laura Addison, who is ninety years old and now very frail. In taking extracts from the text it has been necessary to compress some events and slightly edit other passages for the ease of reading.

The words remain unchanged and still present a vivid narrative of what life was like in the Fens in the latter half of the nineteenth century, during Queen Victoria's reign. Wherever possible I shall let John Thompson speak for himself

ii

My father was a shepherd and his earnings were 12/- a week from 4 o'clock in the morning till 8 o'clock at night. He had seven cows to milk night and morning and a thousand sheep to look after and had to go out with a team of horses in the middle of the day ...

I will tell you now what I have done, what I have heard, what I have seen and what I think. I can remember we used to go gleaning wheat barley beans and peas and I can remember how the corn was threshed with a horse-machine ...

Father had two gallons of milk from the house each day for the family and very often a sheep's head and plucks. He was very often brought a half-drowned sheep which we called drowned mutton and we sometimes had a barley-bread loaf, so you can see how we lived ...

My father also used to take the toll from a toll-gate and it was a penny for a donkey tuppence for a horse and when they had no money they used to throw us coal, turf and logs of wood for the fire. My father also had an eel greg which some call an eel-hive and when he emptied it into a bucket it was full many times ... We fished in the river and often caught large fish weighing 18-20 lbs each – this is what was done in our leisure. My father sat beside us in the summertime and told us that when the wind is in the south it blows the bait into the fishes mouth and when the wind is in the west you catch the biggest and the best, but when the wind is in the north you won't get much broth and when the wind is in the east you will not get a very big feast, and I must tell you that the wind is north-east or south-west the biggest part of the year.

By the time John Thompson was seven years old he was working regularly on the land, crow-scaring, cow-tending, and doing odd jobs, all for fourpence a day,

I can remember being in a gang of twenty or twenty-five and we had to pull every weed with two leaves out of the corn and we'd weed 10-15 acres a day. We had to be in the yard by 6 o'clock in the morning and if we was behind a minute we'd get a kick up the backside or a clout on the head and sent home. I have heard father mob mother a many a time for not getting us off in the morning for we had a mile to walk to work and it used to be a very bad road in winter-time and if we got off the path we'd be up to our knees in slub and water.

In 1863 when John was eight years old there was a total eclipse of the sun at midday so he took all his pigs home because he thought it was night. He then sat down to have his dinner before going to bed. But three hours later he saw that the sun was shining again and he knew then that something was wrong – an error which took some explaining and gave cause for much teasing. The following day one of the 4-week-old pigs in his charge fell into a dyke. The farmer warned him that if that happened again he would drown him. By the age of ten he was earning tenpence a day and learning how to plough,

> In my leisure hours there was always someone ploughing, winter and summer, and I used to go and get hold of the men's ploughs and have ploughed a few rounds with them at my side. By the time I was twelve I could plough as good as a man. The men used to give us boys a penny or tuppence to see who could draw the straightest furrow. I could harrow as straight as I could plough too ...
>
> Now I must tell you about a very sharp Christmas when I can remember a bullock being roasted on the ice and I can tell you too that my mother was washing her pudding cloths in hot water and when she took them out they were all turned to ice.

Like all country women, John Thompson's mother worked as hard as the men. In addition to all the day work and the feeding of a large family, she used to bake fifteen loaves of bread at a time and all the meat pies which she cooked on Sundays. A popular meal then was hare pie. He recalled something that other fenmen had told me, 'The old hares were so numerous in the Fens then that they used to lay about the land in furrows and my father could walk up to them and just pick them up.'

In those days few working-class children received much of a formal education. Schooling had to be paid for and with a large family that was impossible. All the days were the same, Sundays as well as weekdays. The only difference they saw in the year was, he said, in the change of the seasons. At the age of twelve he had to think about leaving home to start work in service,

> My wages were to be two pounds a year and my food for twelve months. I was now a young man and had to act as a young man ... I can remember seeing a corpse going through the village at full gallop and said to my master – are they a bit late for the burial? No, John, he said, Mr Mockson has died with a bad disease, they don't want to keep him long.

This was most likely cholera, which was rife in the Fens in the middle of the nineteenth century.

iii

In 1869, at the age of fourteen, Thompson was told that he would be going a long way from home to work for a Mr Thomas Bass at Sutton St James for six pounds a year and his lodging.

> When I got there I had four cows to milk night and morning and had to drive my Mistress to Long Sutton market on Fridays. I can well remember what I saw one Friday morning before we went to market. As it was a house that had no chambers and they were all low rooms, I see my Mrs in her bedroom and she sat there shaving herself with a razor and I thought this was funny as I'd never seen a woman with whiskies before ... I can also remember that I had to take the wheelbarrow and gather cow-dung when it was dry. I used to stack it in a little round heap close against the back door and my Mrs used to boil the kettle with it and cook the dinner with it to save coal ... There was a man who lived close by in a mud-and-stud house with no chambers and there were great holes all round so you could shove your head through. I said to him once, what have you got that great chaff-riddle up there for? and he said why to stop the wind getting in.

When he was sixteen John took a job in Wisbech Fen with an old man named Robert Penn who had two sons. His wage was now £9 a year plus half a pint of beer every day with his dinner. They all lived in one room. The master and his wife and their two sons sat at one table and the servant girl and John sat at a side table. The masters all had one pint of beer each with their meals and smoked a long pipe in the evenings as they talked over the day's work.

Most of the jobs that John Thompson took seldom lasted more than a year and he was soon 'letting' himself out to other farmers in Outwell, Tilney All Saints, Guyhirn and Marshland Smeeth, where he worked for Mr Charles Hubbard as a second horse-keeper responsible for nine horses. It was to be his ninth job in eight years and the place where he celebrated his twentieth birthday. Whilst there he heard the following story which reflects on some of the practices used by the 'resurrectionists' when body-snatching was common throughout England,

They was going to bury a man from the Workhouse and they reckoned that he had no friends whatever so his body was sent to London but when the coffin got to the churchyard there was a friend drawed up who said this was my grandfather and I will have a look in the coffin to see him for the last time. As there was a carpenter's shop close-by they sent for a screwdriver and the box was opened up and you can imagine their surprise when they found there was no corpse in it at all, only stones. So the man said I will see about this and eventually the corpse came back next day and was buried at 3 o'clock.

The public house in Marshland Smeeth then was The Hickathrift kept by Mr John Mace who had four daughters, none of whom he wanted to get married. But they all did, the third one becoming Mrs Thompson on 8 December 1875. On their wedding day they had a two-mile walk to church and back through a couple of inches of snow,

As we was going home we met fourteen or fifteen men and they had all got a snowball in their hands and I said to my wife we are fearly in it now. One or two chaps stood there with hats for us to put some coppers in but we didn't and so they all said 'shall we snowball them?' Then one called out 'let the weddingers go in peace,' so we came home and our next-door neighbours didn't know we was married till next day.

In 1876 John went to live in Tydd St Giles where he worked for his brother-in-law, who was a thresher. But then came disaster,

A week after Michaelmas, the 18th October, between six and seven o'clock at night, thrashing and clearing up I walked up the drum and stepped on to the "beaters" which smashed my foot and knees all to pieces. It took off a slice of my arms and fingers and it took the men an hour to get me out. They took me to Wisbech hospital around midnight and the doctors said one to another 'He's near death's door – we will not take it off tonight. If he does revive by tomorrow we will take it off then.' Well, they took my left leg off just above my knee and just as they got it off I came round so the doctor said 'Hello my boy, smell of this handkerchief again' so I did and the next time I came round I was in the ward ... I was there three months and had all as your heart could wish for. I was waited on hand and foot and they used to allow me half-a-pint of porter a day with my lunch, dinner and supper so I was looked after better than if I had been at home ... But my father-in-law was very good to us and would tell us there was always a home for us as long as he had one.

iv

His days of farm-work over John Thompson trained himself to be a cobbler and, with his wife's help, was soon well known in the area for both mending and making shoes. They were so successful that eventually they were able to move into their own small house with a garden, which John even managed to dig with only one foot, delighted that he could grow his own vegetables again.

During these years John and his wife became deeply involved in the growth of non-conformist religion in the Fens, particularly the Primitive Methodists. Few working-class people had any time for the Church of England then, which represented the Tory Party and the bosses. If farm-workers voted at all they supported the Liberals and if they were religious they supported the chapels. Soon there was not a village in the Fens without its Methodist, Baptist, or Congregational chapel, most of them with large congregations and choirs. The Thompsons were evangelical in their worship and loved a fiery sermon. Soon John was himself to become a local preacher and received invitations to preach in neighbouring villages. Both he and his wife had a sound knowledge of the scriptures and a profound faith in God,

I will tell you this that we were brought very low once and didn't hardly know where to get a bite of bread so my wife said we were going to spend our last tuppence on a small loaf. Then she got the bible and read a piece of scripture where it said 'I will never see the righteous forsaken nor his seed begging for bread.' I said to her something will come in the morning, and it did. There was a ten-shilling postal-order from some relatives in Middlesborough.

But, on 16 December 1890, a few days before her thirty-ninth birthday, Mrs Thompson died and their short but devoted marriage came to an end,

> These are the last words she said to me – 'Don't weep because I am going home to heaven to meet my Saviour so dry up. If I was going to hell you might weep for me but not now.' Her father stood at her bedside and he told me it was no good stopping at home as this was harvest-time, so we locked her up in the house and left ...

Grief-stricken though he was John went to work and then settled down to looking after himself – not an easy task for a man who had always had so much done for him. He could cope with getting the fire going in the morning and cooking his breakfast but when he returned home at night and the fire was out, when there was no tea ready or anyone to greet him, he became very depressed. A year later he decided to take on a house-keeper. In fact he acquired two – his aunt and her daughter. But he soon found that two housekeepers were worse than none so he 'got shot of' his aunt and wisely kept the niece. The arrangement seemed to work satisfactorily for a time but a few years later John Thompson decided to re-marry and start his own family, of which Mrs Laura Addison was a daughter and eventually the recipient of this story.

With a new life before him John's sense of humour returned and a few pages later in his memoirs he is able to tell some amusing anecdotes. One must surely be among the first 'Irish stories' ever told. This Irishman, who lived in the Fens, was very ill and about to leave this world,

> His wife said I will go out-doors and see what sort of night it is. It was about eleven or twelve o'clock and she came back into the house and said that it was a dark, cold and stormy night for a man to be leaving so why didn't he stop while the morning and see which way to go, which he did ... And there was an old

neighbour of ours who went to an optician's shop in Wisbech to get a new pair of glasses. He fetched her a dozen pair to try on but none of them suited the old lady so he said 'I've got a pair that will' and he goes into another room and brings out a pair that had no glasses in at all. She put them on and said she could see beautifully and bought them.

And it is impossible not to include the story of the mother who wrote to her small son's schoolteacher, saying, 'Pardon me for calling your attention to the fact that you have pulled young Johnnie's right ear so often that it is now longer than the other. Please pull his left ear for a while to oblige his mother.'

v

In 1895 John Thompson paid a visit with his ageing mother to see some relatives in Burton-on-Trent, probably the ones who had sent him ten shillings when he was down to his last twopence. Whilst there he was taken from one brewery to another to see how the beer was made and admitted that he had never seen so much beer in all his life,

> I was there nine days and saw not one man the worse for drink …
> It took eleven trains to take one brewer's labourers to work and
> his name was Mr Bass … Eight or nine-hundred labourers went
> on each train – men, women and children. Each train was
> numbered so they all knew their own trains and I thought to
> myself this was a sight.

Reading this my own thoughts went back to the visit I had made to Elgood's Brewery in Wisbech and of my meeting with Sir Henry Holder, who came from the Midlands brewing industry and would have known scenes like this. But the prospect of 900 labourers arriving at Elgood's each morning was one I do not think he would have wished to contemplate these days.

In the same year, Mr Thompson recorded that on 24 March there was a very severe gale, the worst that the Fens had seen for many years. Thousands of trees were ripped up, hundreds of corn-stacks demolished and many houses damaged.

One of the last entries in this unfinished account of a man's memories was of the death of Queen Victoria on 22 January 1901. With the end of her reign we also come to the end of John

Thompson's story. For an uneducated man he had recalled with unsophisticated clarity and good humour that age of contrasts and slow progress. He would, no doubt, be very surprised and delighted to see some of the changes that have come to the world he knew. At times, reading the words he had dictated to his son, it was possible to believe that I was actually there in the room listening to him myself. No story-teller can ask for a greater compliment than that and perhaps one day the whole of this worthy manuscript will be available for others to enjoy.

John Thompson died on 14 May 1924 at the age of sixty-nine.

12   Knowing Just How Noah Felt

And the waters prevailed and were greatly increased upon the earth … And the waters prevailed upon the earth an hundred and fifty days … And God made a wind to pass over the earth and the waters assuaged.

Genesis

i

It could have been a spring day. Bright, transparent sky, opaque clouds. The fields green and golden. But the wind would not allow that deception for long. It wrinkled the water in the dykes, made the grass on the banks crouch under its weight, and bounced like an invisible water-skier across the Fens. In a nearby field a flock of gulls, like a patch of snow that had forgotten to melt, hugged the earth lest the wind should blow them away one by one. Only the lapwings appeared to be enjoying it as they tumbled in the air with acrobatic skill.

But the wind could not harm the quality of light. It may have improved it, polishing the sky's glass until nothing dulled the colour and outline of everything the eye could see. And for the trained eye there is always plenty to see in the Fens – a distant church, an isolated farmhouse, a derelict barn, the upright of a signpost with no fingers pointing to anywhere, a heron in the reeds, the flash of a stoat crossing the road, and the space!

Who would have guessed that less than a hundred miles away snow was falling, that the road over the Pennines was blocked, and that Scotland was cringing under blizzard conditions and a hurricane. The wind we were getting in the Fens was no more than the wing-tip of the weather front affecting the north of Britain. And how often this happens, that we escape the worst of the winter weather. Whilst much of the country is disappearing under inches of snow we can still be enjoying a day like this. The trouble is that we usually have to suffer from other people's winters, particularly when it comes to flooding. When the snow falls we may be passed over with no more than a light dusting, enough for us to say in years to come, 'It always snowed in January when we were young.' It is when a general thaw sets in that our problems begin, when the melting snows from Bedfordshire, Northamptonshire and Lincolnshire start to pour into our rivers – the Nene, the Welland and the Great Ouse – making it impossible for their banks to contain much longer stampeding waters. When they can't, when those banks break, the fields that were already below the river level, are quickly drowned. The problem is further aggravated if the excess of water flowing into the Fens coincides with high tides coming in from the North Sea. We are then attacked on two fronts and there is little hope of escape.

As we have already seen, and will hear more about in a moment, there is one fear above all others that fills fen people with dread and that is the fear of floods. When the worst happens the work of 300 years can be undone in a couple of days. More damage has been wrought in the Fens by water than by anything else. It is almost as if nature is determined every now and then to win back that which she believes she has lost to the engineers, to the farmers, and the country estates.

For as long as men have been writing about the Fens they have written passionately about floods – Miller and Skertchly, Charles Kingsley and James Wentworth Day among them. It was a subject not lost on novelists such as Dorothy L. Sayers and Graham Swift, or on the poet John Clare, 'From wet week so great an ocean flows / That every village to an island grows ...'

The magnitude of some of those floods can be judged by fenmen referring to them as 'The Great Drowning' or simply 'The Drowned', or even 'The Second Flood' which they put close to the one experienced by Noah. At least he had adequate warning from above to build his Ark and select his stock. Until recent years, with weather satellites and more accurate forecasting, floods could give fenmen very little warning of their rise. River levels could be watched, the volume of water flowing into rivers could be controlled by sluices and pumping stations. What could not always be foretold was the wind factor and some of our worst flooding has always coincided with high winds.

Fenland records show a catalogue of disasters from the thirteenth century to the present day. In earlier years the lack of drainage, or the neglect of what drainage there was, meant that uncontrolled waters had the Fens at their mercy, especially in the winter months when the rivers were already full. Great progress has been made in drainage during the last sixty years but, even with modern engineering, we are not completely safe. Nothing can change the low level of the land and for every million pounds spent on flood-protection a hundred million tons of water must be disposed of or kept in check.

Almost every town and village has its own story to tell – Earith, Somersham, Over, Littleport, Prickwillow, Ely, Wisbech, Parson Drove, Thorney and Crowland. In 1763 an extreme part of the North Level was drowned with great loss of life, cattle and property. Worse followed in 1770, making the land unfarmable for three years. Wisbech is a typical example of how the floods affect everybody. It was flooded almost to extinction in 1571 and 1613, and has come close in every century since. In our own times the floods of 1947, 1963 and 1978 are still talked about by people who were caught up in each drama. As well as their evidence we have old photographs, newspaper cuttings, film archives and the water authorities' official reports to remind us of what horrors can be brought upon us by water. But as often happens in such tragedies the true nature of the people themselves is revealed. Floods have produced in the fenman an heroic defiance and a determination not to be beaten by nature no matter how devastating the event. I shall never forget a man in Littleport telling me,

It wasn't only the water coming off the banks. It seemed to be coming up from underneath the ground as well. I could see my garden rising up and down like that – pumping like a man's heart. That were bloody frightening I can tell you. And then the end of my house blew out, everything washed away ... nothing!

Another man told me how he watched a new three-piece suite caught up in the flood that rushed through his house, the easy chairs and settee washed away like driftwood. 'But it's no good sitting down and howling your eyes out, you just have to get on and do something about it.'

Charles Kingsley, writing in his *Prose Idylls* (1885) said,

> No one has ever seen a fen-bank break without honouring the stern quiet temper which there is in these men, when the north-easter is howling above, the spring-tide roaring outside, the brimming tide-way lapping up to the dyke-top or flying over in sheets of spray; when round the one fatal thread which is trickling over the dyke, hundreds of men are clustered, without tumult, without complaint, marshalled under their employers, fighting the brute powers of nature, not for their employer's sake alone, but for the sake of their own year's labour and their own year's bread. The sheep have been driven off the land below; the cattle stand shivering on high dykes inland; they will be saved in punts if the worst befall. But a hundred spades, wielded by practised hands, cannot stop that trickle. The trickle becomes a rush, the rush a roaring waterfall. The dyke-top trembles – gives. The men makes efforts, desperate, dangerous, as of sailors in a wreck, with faggots, hurdles, sedge, turf; but the bank will break, and slowly they draw off; sullen, but uncomplaining, beaten, but not conquered … He who sees, as I have seen, a sight like that, will repine no more that the primaeval forest is cut down, the fair mere drained. For instead of mammoth and urus, stag and goat, that fen now feeds cattle many times more numerous than all the wild venison of the primaeval jungle; and produces crops capable of nourishing a hundred times as many human beings; and more – it produces men a hundred times as numerous as ever it produced before, more healthy and long-lived – and if they will, more virtuous and more happy – than ever was Girvian in his log-canoe, or holy hermit in his cell. So we, who knew the deep fen, will breathe one sigh over the last scrap of wilderness and say no more.

Kingsley could have been writing that about the Fens a hundred years later for I know he would have found the fenmen more healthy if not more happy and still as determined to keep the land dry as they were then. What that author does achieve is a concentration of the whole history of the Fens into one paragraph.

I also heard more first-hand descriptions of the 1947 floods when I listened to the tape-recordings from the Farmland Museum Sound Archives at Haddenham. George Amory remembered them vividly,

The true horror of the floods became clear

We had more 'n ten feet of water in the land then. No, more than
that. It must have been near fourteen feet, with waves washing
over tackle, out-buildings and the tops of bungalows ... I
remember that Fred Palmer had four big corn-stacks in one of
his fields. One Sunday night we were looking across the Fen and
I said, 'Do you know what! That stack's a-moving,' and they all
said don't talk stupid! But it was. The stack floated away on the
flood and moved with the wind. It turned round and swam back
across the Fen ... That was a sight I can tell yer.

Later, when the true horror of those floods became clear,

George knew that Haddenham would not be spared, at least not in the Fen,

When the bank blowed at Over Fen it drowned all the Fen ... I went along that night, me and my wife, and we met Perse Allen. There was already a hole nearly thirty-foot long in the bank and I'll tell you the words that I said to him, I said, 'Perse, you can flit!' And he said whatever are you talking about and I said, 'That'll fill Over Fen and come over the road and fill Hill Row Fen too.' And it did ... It went on all night. You could hear it roaring miles away. It filled up all the Fen from Sutton to Stretham, four miles across. It were like a sea. Water! Water! Then the sight-seers came in their thousands to have a look at it and the police had to turn 'em back. The place was bunged-up with traffic ... I tell you what – we didn't like to see it but it did Hill Row Fen good, because afore that flood there used to be three different kinds of soil in them fields – one we called marley and that would only grow special things like wazzles [mangel-wurzels]. The other would only grow weeds and the rest a bit of barley. But after the floods that soil all became the same and would grow anything. The water did it good. It did the farmers good, too. Some of 'em did very well out of it ... Most of the distressed people got new households. The old wooden farm buildings which were rotting away were replaced by brick buildings. It was like getting a new farm. In the heart of the Fen where they'd lost everything they did very well. They were fitted out with new rugs and chairs which had been lost – at least they said they were. Before the flood you could go into a farm-labourer's cottage and the only hearth-rug they had on the floor was a clean bag, you know, a corn-sack. But after the flood they had new posh carpets and furniture ... They were well satisfied – and it takes a lot to satisfy a farmer ... But it was a heartbreaking sight, I can tell you. You felt so helpless. There was this water coming at you at about walking pace, which was too fast for us to get everything moved, but what could we do? In some ways that land still belongs to the sea and when she claims her own you can't do much to stop it. And that's that. Some of the water stayed on the land for three months. I had only about two acres clear and I grew cauliflowers on that, the first time I'd ever grown cauliflowers in my life.

George Aamory died a couple of years ago but he left behind some priceless memories of ninety years in the Fens and, contrary to the commonly held opinion about fenmen, he was never lost for a word. Indeed, like all true men of the Fens he was a natural story-teller. Unfortunately, what you cannot capture on the printed page is all the arm-waving and gesticulating that goes into the telling.

In thinking again of the floods, which are always reminders of what the land was once like, I think also of the men who helped to drain the Fens, the river-makers who received scant reward for their labours and had no idea how wealthy the reclaimed land was to become.

> The dyker who with muscle and spade
> Cleaved a life-line in a barren land,
> Gave also of his manliness to make
> Grain grow where water had been paramount.
>
> How blindly did he work to one man's plan
> To drain the wildfowls' roosting-place?
> As bones ached with the winter's cramp

Did he smell the wealth that would never be his?

More often he went to his bed with eyes
Clouded by ooze from a dying fen.
No coins clutched in arthritic hands,
No lark-song lifting his head to the sun.

Grown old with delving, wracked with damp,
He'd barely strength to leave his seed
In the unwilling womb. And when he did
His child cried with the fears of darkness in its head.

But he and a thousand of his kind
Were the beginnings and makers of this earth
Which fed men's children for three hundred years
And put this praising in my breath.

Before these fields are drowned by iron and brick,
Or farms become a new world's wilderness,
Let these words ring in furrows for a man
Who first made rivers glisten with December stars.

ii

When I started out on this chapter I never expected such a
sudden change of mood to take place. I was all for spring and
bright days, for a land flowing with the young green shoots of a
new year, rather than reminders of floods or drainage. But once
those subjects get into your mind it is not easy to dismiss them
and it is not a bad thing to be jolted out of complacency
sometimes. If those blizzards now raging across Scotland were
to come south, if a quick thaw overfilled our rivers again, then
the scenes with which I began this chapter would be erased by a
much grimmer picture. As with everything else in the Fens,
there is nowhere to hide. The days exist on a fragile web that
trembles in the wind. We hold on, making the most of what is
given. If the fenman sometimes appears taciturn it is because he
is aware of his frailty in nature. As the man in Littleport said to
me when I asked him if anything like the 1947 floods could
happen again, 'You dursen't open your mouth too soon.'

But, as I made my way home through Ramsey and Holm Fen,
the day itself had not been spoilt by these thoughts. The light

was still good, the fields breathing, the trees on Holme Fen Nature Reserve now shaking starlings out of their branches like black seeds from their pods. And how can I pass that place without stopping to enjoy again that ancient smell of the Fens that still lingers on after the Mere was drained?

13 On Even the Bleakest
of Winter Days

... There are other places which also are at the world's end.

T.S. Eliot

*Nowhere that I have been to in the world does the land fade into
the sea so inconspicuously ... You cannot say where one begins
and the other ends.*

Hilaire Belloc

i

If you want to know what it feels like to go to the edge of the
world you need do no more than drive over Gedney Marsh to
Gedney Drove End and walk along the last footpath between
civilization and the North Sea, especially in winter when a gale is
blowing and you are staring into the wind's jaws. Behind you,
fifteen to twenty feet below the level of the path, are the fields
which were stolen from the sea. At this time of the year they are
often waterlogged and sulk in some primordial state defying
fertility. In front of you are the slimy mud-flats, the glistening
creeks, and then the sea – the brown, turgid sea of the Wash
which has received the waters from the rivers Welland, Nene
and the Great Ouse, mixing them in with the North Sea that
looks as menacing today as it must have done when the Vikings
invaded these shores more than a thousand years ago. The
coastline then was much further inland but you can see how
easily the long-boats from Scandanavia would have made their
way into the Fens to destroy the abbeys of Crowland,
Medeshamstede, and much else besides.

I was standing on dry land which had once been under the
sea, walking a causeway over the shadows of water, over the

buried waves that could not return to the tide. The wind was so strong you could lean on it. It was like putting your shoulder to a door that would not open. Above me two fighter planes chased each other in mock-battle or attacked targets in the creeks. After a few minutes the wind must have blown them away because they disappeared, leaving only the warning cries of birds who had seen us arrive – the redshanks, curlews and lapwings that were wading in the shining mud.

Beyond the Wash I could see the coast of north Norfolk and, much closer, the lighthouses at Guy's Head. It is such a difficult area to describe because it really is neither sea nor land. It is a kind of unmade, unclaimed, forgotten kingdom, frequented mostly by wildfowlers who enjoy these conditions. If the eye can penetrate beyond the far skyline you are looking down the wind-paths taken by the cold air blown in from Northern Russia. For some it is an anonymous landscape that can never beguile. Its character is more introvert than that of the Cambridgeshire Fens and I have to admit that my own feelings about it are of respect rather than admiration. But it is an important part of the fen country that cannot be ignored and the more often I visit it the more I appreciate its remoteness and atmosphere. It hasn't changed much since Hilaire Belloc came here at the turn of the century and described his visit in *The Hills and the Sea* (1906). After telling of an amusing scene at Sutton Bridge, where he and a companion were unable to cross the bridge over the Nene – 'that monstrous thing of iron standing poised upon a huge pivot in midstream' – because it was being cleaned by an insignificant little man 'with a little rag', he wrote,

Along the cut which takes the Nene out to sea, then across some level fields, and jumping a ditch or two, one gets to the straight, steep, and high dyke which protects the dry land and cuts off the plough from the sea marshes. When I had climbed it and looked out over endless flats to the sails under the brune of the horizon, I understood the Fens ... You have but to eliminate that embankment to imagine what the whole countryside must have looked like before it was raised, and the meaning of the Fens becomes clear to you. The Fens were long ago but the continuation inland of this sea morass ... But man, religious or greedy, or just wandering, crept in after each inundation and began to tame the water and spread out even here his slow interminable conquest.

Man has undoubtedly built in his time some very strange mixtures of houses, from the narrow, mean and ugly to the grand and opulent. But Belloc's excitement is still an easy one to share. A walk along the embankment gives you a feeling of striding between two worlds which are somehow held together by your own presence there. And I always find it satisfying at Guy's Head to walk where the River Nene reaches the end of its journey through the fens because I know then that I have then followed its route all the way and in every season.

ii

A few days later I was back on the banks of the Nene and the sea-wall. The wind now blew from the north and it was several degrees colder. The tide was in and there was much more water in the Wash. The river itself was in turmoil, churned up by currents and aggravated by the gale. Ahead of me the sky was already funereal black and it was difficult to see where earth and clouds met. This exposed landscape has often endured wildness but it never ceases to alarm anyone who is experiencing these uncompromising elements in nature either for the first time, or again. We are shown many times what fragile creatures we are and to take on these marshes you need to be very courageous or foolish. It was a day on which you could expect sinister things to happen.

When the rain's avalanche arrived it was time to take cover and to think of getting home. Not even a wildfowler would want to be out on the marshes today, not only for his own safety but because no birds would be on the wing in such weather.

I drove back through Dawsmere, Holbeach St Mark and Holbeach St Matthew, then down to Moulton Seas End, Whaplode, Postland and Thorney, still pursued by those menacing clouds which were determined to see me off their land. Litter and large twigs were blown across the roads. Pub-signs swung and creaked. Gates were pushed open by invisible hands. There was an atmosphere of impending doom as if we were about to witness the last winter on earth.

iii

'Winter? You say you want to know what I think about winter?'

said an 82-year-old man to me one day as we sat in a pub round
a smouldering fire. Before I could reply he thrust out his knotted
hands that had been clutching his walking-stick and said,

> That's what I think about winter. Years a-working on wet land,
> years of stooping over rows of taters in a biting wind, of getting
> wet through day after day until you thought you'd never bloody
> stand up straight again. Carrot-pulling, beet-chopping, tater-
> riddling, and ploughing. I used to go 'um some nights when my
> hands were that bloody cracked and swollen that I couldn't
> unlace my boots. The missus had to do that for me. Fifty-six
> years I worked on the land and a fat lot of thanks I got for it, too.
> That's what I think about winter.

The customer next to him said, 'And you just couldn't git into a
nice hot bath either when you got 'ome, could you? Not like the
young 'uns do today.'

> Bath? You must be joking. You were lucky if you got a bath once
> a week then. We didn't have no bathroom or central-heating. We
> boiled the water outside in a copper and carried it to a bath in the
> kitchen, then we got in one arter the other. And I can tell you
> that the water might have been a bit thick by the time we'd
> finished but we were all clean.

For the next few minutes the subject for everyone stayed with
baths; where they had them, when they had them, and why they
had them. Then, the glasses were refilled and the conversation
continued as before. One of the men told me,

> My father never bathed at all in winter if he could help it. He
> hardly ever took his clothes off. 'Blast me, boy,' he'd say, 'I've
> only just got meself warm and I don't intend to get frez all over
> again just to have a bath. It's only me hands what get mucky and I
> can wash them under the tap,' which is what he did. And I'll tell
> you another thing, he never caught a cold all winter.

Each of the men had worked on the land, some for much longer
than others, and I was beginning to feel that I still retained a
distinctly romantic view of winter, especially when they
described some of the damp cottages in which they had been
forced to live. One spoke of icicles hanging down the bedroom
walls and another of a roof patched up with cardboard. 'The

farmers didn't care too much in them days how we lived as long as they were all right.' I was not wholly unaware of what winters used to be like years ago when working people's homes had fewer comforts and most manual labourers were exposed much more to the weathers. My own parents and grandparents had worked on the land and I had heard them talk of what conditions were like. I had seen too many generations crippled with rheumatism and arthritis to be blind to what winter could do to a body faced with the seasons 'conspiracies'.

Story-tellers are competitive creatures and when I asked the men what they could remember about winter nights seventy years or more ago I soon had them interrupting each other before anyone completed what was begun.

'I can say that the only light we had then was a lantern and that very likely was no more than a candle in a jam-jar.'

'But you didn't need a light in them days. You could walk blindfold then 'cus you knew every bump of the road.'

'And what's more you knew who else'd be on it. You can't do that nowadays. There's bound to be some mad bloody lunatic tearing along at ninety miles an hour, even at two o'clock in the morning.'

'But don't get any idea that we buried ouselves indoors every night just 'cus it were winter. There was allus plenty to do.'

That plenty to do included going to the pub most evenings to play cards, darts or dominoes, going to band-practice (there were dozens of brass bands in the Fens then), or simply visiting relatives who needed a hand with putting up some shelving, or killing and plucking some chickens for Christmas.

Then one of the men surprised me by saying,

I liked winter best of all when I was young, especially if it was a hard winter. Myself, I think the land needs a good few weeks of frost, and so do we. Much better'n all that damp. when that gits into your bones you feel that wizened up you can hardly move.

And didn't want to either. I can remember when you couldn't budge my father away from the fire once he'd sat down. He used to stand his mug of beer on the hearth, heat the poker and then stick it into his beer to warm it up. 'I've got to get comfort into my bones somehow,' he'd say.

At least when we got a good hard winter we could git in a bit of skating. That used to warm us up, too.

And, as if suddenly turning at the end of ploughing a furrow, the conversation switched to skating. How they learnt, where they learnt, who they beat, how thick the ice used to be. Who were the best skaters they had seen. I had heard it all before and, as always, was assured that there would never again be fenland skaters like there were, once upon a time. Legends. The men still lived on legends. Their eyes glowed. The fires of their youth burned brightly as their deeds were recalled. So it was for their fathers and, because they could tell their own tales, we now have a treasury of memories that may never be surpassed.

And what about Christmas, I asked. Did they have any special memories about that?

> Well, as far as I can remember, Christmas Day was hardly any different from any other. If you worked with horses you went to work just like you did every day. They needed feeding and looking after. Same with cows. You couldn't leave the poor buggers to go unmilked for a couple of days just because it was Christmas.
>
> We sometimes got a bit extra to eat, like a good cockerel and a basin of brawn, or some brandy pudding. But there were not many presents.

The man who disliked winter so bitterly told me:

> I can remember on one occasion we didn't get a bloody thing. It was as much as my poor old parents could do to scratch a meal together, let alone give us presents. My father hadn't worked for sixteen weeks, we owed ten weeks' rent at half a crown a week, and the youngest child had just died of pneumonia at the age of two. There was no point in anybody wishing us a very merry Christmas 'cus we knew we wouldn't get one.
>
> There were more important things in life than that then, weren't there? I think they make far too much fuss over a couple of days. It's the rest of the year you've got to bother about.

I thought that it might be worth getting them to talk about politics but already they were looking at the clock and mumbling something about 'toddling off'. 'Better not keep the beef-pudden waiting, Charlie.'

'No, nor the missus. I promised to take her to a whist drive this afternoon.' One by one they politely wished me a good day and left.

iv

As I drove away I was reminded of a more embarrassing moment some two or three years ago when I called at another pub not far from the Wash. I had volunteered to go to a theatrical warehouse in Boston to collect a tailor's female dummy which was needed for a drowning scene in a film that was being made about the novelist L.P. Hartley. What the director did not tell me was that the model would be naked, nor could the suppliers find anything to wrap her in for the journey back to Crowland. It was a fairly up-to-date model which did not try to disguise the female anatomy. Having carried her through the streets to my parked car (which I could not get near to the warehouse because of major roadworks) I found she would not fit into the car boot. The back seat was already full of other props and so I twisted her into a sitting position and put her in the front seat next to me. Not wanting to break the law I also fixed her seat-belt for her and drove off, noticing that a few Bostonians were still looking very suspiciously at me. It was, I must add, a very hot day. All went well *en route* until I felt like something to eat and, as it was lunch-time, I decided to call at the next decent-looking pub for a bar meal. This happened to be The Mermaid at Surfleet, which was on the right-hand side of the road. In order to cross over I had to wait for a space in the long line of on-coming traffic. After a few lorries had passed I began to notice the drivers slowing down and peering through my windscreen at my un-clad passenger. My waiting was also long enough for the customers in the pub to peer out and wonder whether the young lady would enter the bar like that. I tried to drape something round her but it was too late. When, with relief, I walked into the pub and ordered a cool Guinness, the landlord said something like, 'You're not leaving the girlfriend outside, are you, sir?'

By the time I reached the film crew at Crowland I had received more attention and horn-hooting on one journey than in the whole of my thirty years as a driver. Whether my female model would have had such a look of reality on a winter's day it is hard to say and I am still not sure what explanation I would have given the police if I'd been stopped. When the poor girl was eventually drowned I had mixed feelings. I was grateful to be relieved of the embarrassment and my guilt-complex, but sorry to see the abused lady come to such an unromantic end. As the drowning scene was eventually cut out of the film anyway I felt my moment of notoriety had a bitter-sweet taste to it.

I only related this little incident to show that there is a lighter side to life in the Fens and that the memory of an adventure like that can brighten even the bleakest of winter days.

I once knew a fisherman and a wild-fowler in these parts who claimed he had taken archbishops out fishing in the Wash.

> I tried to drown one or two of 'em but they allus floated to the surface again. I took an ordinary bishop and his friends once but all they wanted to do was to drink bottles of champagne. They didn't seem to be very interested in the fishing. Mind you, neither was I by the time we'd finished … But it's the shooting I like best – and do you know what, some of the best shoots I've been on have been when only a few birds were shot. I don't believe in wholesale slaughter. It's picking off the ones you want that proves whether you're any good or not… After all, I'm very fond of birds.

The amazing, incomprehensible fact is that most of the wild-fowlers I have met express the same sentiments. They love nature, they love birds, and they love the solitude to be found out on those haunting acres which can never be fenced in by man or put under the plough. I'm not sure this was always so for some of the accounts I have read of shoots in the past, especially in the nineteenth century, show a disturbing tally of dead birds – a subject I shall return to later. For the last few days the birds have been lucky.

14 Some Enchanted Evening, or Other

If I had my life to live over again I would have made a rule to read some poetry and listen to some music at least once a week, for perhaps the parts of my brain now atrophied would thus have been kept active through use.

Charles Darwin

'There is a delight in singing though none hear beside the singer.

Walter Savage Landor

i

What do people do with themselves at night in the winter, especially in the Fens? The answer to that question must be the same as it would be in any other part of the country. Many of them stay at home to watch television; many go to a variety of evening classes, or attend indoor sporting activities; others go to Evergreen Clubs, Women's Institutes or whist drives, and some go bell-ringing or to sing in choirs. You only have to read the 'What's On' column in any local newspaper to realize that there is no reason why anyone should be bored and not everyone is letting their brains atrophy for want of use. Admittedly a large number of these pursuits are not restricted to the winter months but I do believe a greater level of enthusiasm is called for to turn up regularly each week for rehearsals or meetings during this time.

I have been associated with Adult Education as a part-time lecturer for over thirty years and I must say that some of those night-time journeys have tested my love of the Fens as well as my love for the subject. Twelve weeks or more driving to some isolated village hall or schoolroom, which may or may not be heated when you get there, is an ordeal that can be very trying for students and tutor. Most of the country roads will be unlit, it might be pouring with rain, or it could be foggy or blowing a gale, but you still have to get there. I have been to speak at Women's Institutes in places so remote that the only square of light on the landscape is the room where the ladies are patiently waiting for their guest to arrive. I have struggled through snow to Pinchbeck, through fog to Long Sutton, slid and slithered my way to Ramsey St Mary's, or relied on fate to get me along Forty Foot to Chatteris – and, usually, it has all been worth it because others have made the effort as well. Whether it's being huddled round a table in Crowland Library studying Virginia Woolf, or competing with a youth club in some community centre whilst trying to discuss Dostoevsky's *Crime and Punishment*, there's a sense of adventure, for the mind as well as the body.

I was talking a few weeks ago to a keen campanologist who has been bell-ringing for nearly forty years. What kept him going, not just on Sundays but at bell-ringing practice every Thursday evening in a cold, draughty, dimly lit church in the Fens? He told me that he enjoyed the company of the rest of the team, that it helped him to keep fit, but above all he loved the sound of bells. 'When you get a good peal going and you know it's being heard miles away, that gives you a feeling of satisfaction, knowing you're doing something that's been going on for hundreds of years. I've always liked the sound of bells across the countryside, especially on a winter's night when the air is still. Don't you?' I agreed that bells at a distance could sound very attractive but doubted if I could spend three or four hours with them in a church tower. I remember some years ago giving a poetry reading in a church where the organizers had forgotten to tell the bell-ringers that there was another event on that evening. But they had turned up for their practice and were determined to go ahead with it because they had a wedding on Saturday afternoon and still couldn't get the changes right. I think some compromise was reached. I read the loud poems while they rang, and the quiet ones while they rested or went outside for a smoke. The ancient art of bell-ringing is a complex one, as Dorothy L. Sayers was able to show in her novel *The Nine Tailors* and those of us who do not understand its skills may not appreciate the subtleties of its music.

ii

Music of another kind which is easier to take at close quarters is singing and one group of musicians that I have been specially interested in during the past year or so is the Peterborough Male Voice Choir. Not only do they sing for pleasure but they also raise thousands of pounds for charities, especially hospitals, contributing generously to laser appeals, scanners, kidney-machines, Children's Hospitals and the Macmillan Centres.

The choir's origins go back to the 1930s when some seasonal workers from Wales arrived at the city's sugar-beet factory and, feeling homesick, decided to form a choir. It was originally called The Nene Valley Singers and had the distinction of appearing with such famous musical personalities as Kathleen Ferrier and the organist Sandy MacPherson. But, as sometimes happens, their membership gradually declined to six and the tradition of male-voice singing looked almost at an end. But a few old stalwarts were not prepared to let this happen. With one or two false starts the choir was reborn to become the present ensemble – sartorially clad in blue blazers and choir ties, some with more developed diaphragms than others, and all expertly organized by the Committee. And, to prove they are not 'M.C.Ps', they now have a lady conductor and a lady accompanist, which is just as well for they can behave like a lot of rowdy sixth-formers ragging each other after a rugger match – not that many of them could play that game now! Perhaps it would be kinder to say they are just a nice bunch of chaps having a few high jinks until it's time to sing. And when they do they are immediately transformed into sensitive, responsive musicians making a beautiful sound as they sing 'Softly As I Leave You', or 'Solitaire'. Then butter wouldn't melt in their mouths. They sing wherever they are asked to and are in great demand. They sing in pubs, formally or informally, in village halls, old people's homes, churches and shopping centres, sometimes to audiences of two or three dozen, sometimes to hundreds and on one occasion to thousands. It would be more accurate to say that they sang *with* thousands when they took part in a massed choir event at Cardiff Arms Park – the biggest male voice choir ever assembled. For successive years they have won the Morriston Orpheus Trophy at the South Woodham Ferrers Male Voice

Choir Festival and, in 1992, were the host choir for a magnificent concert of voice and brass in Peterborough Cathedral. But these great occasions do not diminish their enthusiasm for the less auspicious events at which they raise most of their money for charity.

I decided to follow them around during a typical winter season, to see what they got up to – away from the public eye as well as on stage. To begin with I had to ask myself what sort of men decide to join a male voice choir, and why? Is it to regain, however briefly, that state of 'single blessedness' they enjoyed as bachelors, or to recapture the slightly macho image of a musical rugger-club? No, for some of them are still single and, if not, their wives are often not far away, working in the background selling tickets, cassettes, providing refreshments, making sure that their husbands have the right shirt and tie on, and arrive at the right place on time. Some choir members have been known to turn up at the wrong church, even the wrong village. They really do need looking after.

But who are they? And why are they prepared to give up at least one night a week for rehearsals and one or two others for concerts? It is, after all, voluntary, and at times, expensive. One obvious answer is that they love singing, expressing that need in the words of Alfred, Lord Tennyson, 'I do sing because I must!' Another is that they enjoy comradeship and clearly thrive on all the leg-pulling that is an essential part of choir life. As a choir they are one body of men with a common interest. But all groups are made up of individuals, so what do the members do when they are not singing? Their professions and backgrounds are as wide as you can imagine. They range from builders to bank managers, from schoolteachers to tax collectors, from apprentices to those who are retired. They come not only from the local area but also from Wales, Yorkshire and Norfolk. Some have had previous choir experience, others are new to the game. One singer joined because his children said he sang like Caruso. He said to them, 'I had no idea you knew about Caruso!' They sighed, 'Dad, everybody knows about Robinson Caruso!'

The choir has its own court jester and several natural jokers who keep up the spirits of the rest if needed. As visits to the pub seem to be a condition of membership the services of the jokers are seldom required, but that doesn't stop them and their services must be seen as a bonus. 'It's the only bonus we'll get,' said one of the tenors, continuing the sarcastic rivalry that exists between the tenors, baritones and basses. In fact, the more I know them the more I am coming to the conclusion that a man's sense of humour depends on his range of voice.

I have eavesdropped on a few of their anecdotes about each other. At one rehearsal, for instance, a first-tenor who was afraid of missing a particularly high note was told by the conductor to 'aim above it and then land on top of it'. With new concern he asked what would happen if he missed it on the way down? Before the conductor could reassure him that it would work, one of the basses said, 'You'll end up a counter-tenor, of course!' On another occasion it was suggested that they should organize a sponsored sing to raise money for the funds. 'Each member,' said the secretary, 'should get himself sponsored for singing so many hours without repeating himself or making a mistake.' I think it was one of the baritones who decided to be a street-busker one Saturday afternoon as part of his contribution. All went well until one passer-by stopped and said, 'With a voice like that you should think of joining a choir.' I also heard of how one of the basses had been hypnotized into singing the right notes and didn't make a single mistake, until he woke up.

A concert by the choir does not consist entirely of songs. They have their own impersonators of Stanley Holloway and Max Boyce, and a virtuoso of the Norfolk dialect who, as one choir member suggested, should always carry a translator with him.

The spirit of the choir is summed up in the words of one of its newer members, 'Every performance that we do is enjoyable but there are special moments, like performing in old people's homes and watching the old folk come to life when they join us in singing their favourite songs.' Having sat with the residents of such a home while the choir entertained them, I can share something of that pleasure. Wrinkled faces grow young again, weary eyes light up, and weak voices tremble in the refrain of a song that was popular when they were young. There are tears too, as you see the years fly back to earlier loves, to memories that the music helps to restore, and you see again for a moment the brief glimmer of joy that the song has given. Music restores. Charles Kingsley described the power of music splendidly when he wrote,

There is something very wonderful in music. Words are wonderful enough; but music is even more wonderful. It speaks not to our thoughts as words do; it speaks straight to our hearts and spirits, to the very core and root of our souls ... it is a language by itself, just as perfect in its way, as speech, as words; just as divine, just as blessed.

I have watched the way people respond to music, whether it has been in a cold and dimly lit church where the choir has gone to sing in aid of the restoration fund, or in a city nursing home. I have watched the choir carol-singing in a shopping centre and have joined with them in concerts given in the Key Theatre, Peterborough. I have stood in the crowd and been behind the scenes, and always their joy in giving, in making music, has been an inspiration. Whatever the occasion, the weather or the place, these 'stout-hearted men' – for that is their signature tune – are the cause of far more happiness than havoc. In performance their musicianship and deportment are exemplary, but, oh dear, away from the watchful eye of their musical director, Mrs Freda Woodhouse, they are back to their old schoolboy tricks and tap-room *bonhomie*!

iii

I remember during the interval of one concert talking to an elderly lady who had been joining in several of the songs. Do you have any favourites I asked. 'I like "Some Enchanted Evening" and the Spirituals ... I used to sing in a choir when I was young. You never forget.'

And winter? I asked. Did she mind the winter? 'It's not the cold or the wet I mind so much now, it's the dark. I hate the dark mornings and the dark evenings. It makes the nights so long. They draw the curtains here and put the lights on by four o'clock and it's eight o'clock in the morning before you can see it's daylight.'

Do you ever get out?

Yes. I've got a daughter who lives twelve miles away and she takes me shopping with her sometimes. I like to see all the shops decorated for Christmas but I don't know how people manage these days with some of the prices. When I see what some of them have to pay just to feed their families I'm not sorry that I've only got myself to think about now. Not even that sometimes. They do everything here for you. When I had a young family I could have fed them for six months on what the mothers have to spend in a week, perhaps more.

The choir returned to the stage and the audience settled down to hear 'Autumn Leaves', 'The Windmills of Your Mind, 'Rock-a-my-Soul', and 'Love, Could I Only Tell Thee'. Heads nodded to the music, eyes filled with sadness, then the sounds died away. Outside, it was pouring with rain. I declined the invitation to join the choir for a drink at a nearby pub, and walked slowly home.

At another concert I talked with a lady who saw herself as a 'young 90' and she spoke of the tremendous contribution that was once made to choirs, and music-making generally, by the chapels.

I've been a Methodist all my life and still sing, after a fashion. When I first came to the Fens there were some good choirs, which was a bit of a surprise really, coming from the north where we reckon to have all the good singers. The choir I joined was forty strong and we had one of the best organists for miles. We'd sometimes combine with some of the other chapel choirs and give a performance of Handel's 'Messiah' that was nigh-on as good as the Huddersfield's. Sadly that's all gone now and most of the buildings have been pulled down for office development, or carparks. A great tragedy.

I heard also of some of the smaller chapels where the music was not quite as professional. The organist at one of these was a lady in her eighties and stone deaf. The minister made an arrangement with her that he would always give her a certain sign when it was time to play. He would raise his right hand in the air and then point to the clock. It worked splendidly until one Sunday evening when this particular gesture inadvertently came into his sermon, at which point the lady organist started to play the next hymn. As she never played very loudly he let her continue throughout the sermon, thinking that the background music added a rather novel effect. But when it came to the last hymn the organist had already gone home, believing that she had played all the hymns required that evening. It amused the congregation for a while and they were happy for her to play for another year or more, even though others more capable were willing to take over.

What do people do with themselves at night in winter? There are almost as many answers as there are people. But if they do nothing they are missing something very valuable in life, especially if it means giving pleasure to others, either by performing or providing company.

One of my friends said, 'I bet you're going to call this chapter 'The Fens Are Alive with the Sound of Music' – as if I'd dare! Mind you, I think I came close.

15   What a Way to Spend Saturday

What is all knowledge too but recorded experience, and a product
of history; of which, therefore, reasoning and belief no less than
action and passion, are essential materials?

Thomas Carlyle

One half of the world cannot understand the pleasure of the
other.

Jane Austen

i

While half the male population today is watching football the
other half, so I am told, will be trying to catch fish of one sort or
another. In fact, I think it is true to say that more men will be
sitting on river-banks than on the terraces of football grounds;
more eyes will be on the twitch of a float than on a ball hopefully
going into the net. On a day like this they are welcome to either.

I have been to only one professional football match in my life
and suffered the embarrassment of wearing the wrong coloured
scarf and woolly hat, which I had borrowed for the occasion.
Unfortunately it was an 'away' match and the team I was
supposed to be supporting had been required to change its
colours because the 'home' team wore the same blue and white
strip as ours. So, inadvertently, I found myself dressed for the
opposition and was not very popular with the regular followers
who had known what to do. *They* were all in red and white. As
our team lost I felt the burden of guilt on my shoulders as we sat
in the train bringing us back home. I never went again.

I also have to admit that I have not been fishing all that many
more times than I have been to a football match but I am at least
more familiar with rivers and do know a little about the art that
Izaac Walton immortalized in literature.

Which brings me to the subject I should be writing about in this chapter. As well as the many thousands who will be engaged in some kind of sport today, as well as the weary thousands who will be involved in shopping, odd-jobbing, or whatever tasks winter will allow, a few will be sitting quietly in classrooms, attending one-day Schools or weekend courses on a variety of topics – 'Church Architecture', 'The Civil War', 'The Age of Steam' or, in my case, 'Legends and Literature of the Fens'.

Let me set the scene. It is a cold, foggy February day, one that would certainly not encourage you to pursue any of the outdoor activities available on Saturdays. The college of adult education, where we are to spend our day is a late Victorian school-building with glazed brick walls and high windows – reminiscent of those classrooms some of us may remember attending more than fifty years ago, classrooms with open fires and the smells of ink, chalk, and perhaps polish. The room we are in is warm and well lit, the small tables have been arranged in a semi-informal horseshoe facing the tutor. I have no idea who my students for the day will be until they arrive. A one-day school is always a bit of a gamble and six hours can either go very quickly or seem an exhaustingly long time. I sit looking out of the windows at the grey furry sky, wondering if the weather will prevent any of the people who have enrolled from attending. And, for those who do make it, what will they expect?

Two by two they enter the room as though it were destined to become an ark that might never see dry land again. There are a few familiar faces but most are strangers, looking as nervous as I feel. One elderly lady says, 'I've only come to listen so you won't ask me any questions, will you!' Another says, 'We won't have to do any writing will we?' The seats furthest away from me are filled first.

What a dreary day to be talking about those great fenland spaces, those mighty skies and distant horizons. What a day to be convincing others of the lowlands' subtle beauty and quality of light. I am reminded of an occasion when I took a coach-party round the Fens on an autumn Sunday afternoon when nothing beyond the steamed-up windows could be seen and all my enthusiasm had to be accepted without proof. At least we shall have the written proof of others in front of us today and, hopefully, some members of the group will have seen the landscape on better days.

But who are these seventeen people assembled before me? And why are they here? I find there are two or three married couples, several wives – looking forward no doubt to their day of 'single blessedness', and a few people who are still single. There are teachers, office-workers, a social worker, a retired builder, and a farmer's daughter. Some originate from Ireland, some from Yorkshire, London or Norfolk, and just one or two admit to being 'local', i.e. born and bred fen-dwellers.

ii

W.G. Hoskins maintained in his *The Making of the English Landscape*, that we can never fully understand a landscape until we know something of its history. So perhaps for those who do not know why the Fens are *what* they are it is necessary to go back to an age which resulted in their creation. It is necessary to go back 10,000 years to when thick layers of ice still covered much of what is now northern Europe and our climate was nearer to that of the Arctic Circle. The Fens, as we know them today, did not exist. There was no North Sea or British Isles. Our three main rivers – the Great Ouse, Nene, and Welland were no more than tributaries of the River Rhine and we were undeniably part of the continental land mass which is now Europe. It was possible then for animals from the eastern regions of that continent to make their way over to this country, which is why, when the first settlers came here they would have known bears, bison, tigers, wolves and even elephants. But they were not as old as the earliest animals which must have walked here once. Skeletons of prehistoric beasts have been found embedded in the clay that was the deposit of the Jurassic sea which takes us back to nearly 200 million years ago. We continue briefly with the last ice age and the great thaw, when huge packs of ice started grinding the land into valleys, when the frozen snows began to melt, creating new seas to separate the British Isles from the mainland. Left on these islands were those primitive people who were to become the first Britons. Tribes were established, nations born, kings and warriors emerged to fight over each other's kingdoms and eventually lead their subjects into the future. The Fen country then was mostly marsh and mere, a sunken bowl which was soon to become what Daniel Defoe called 'the sink of thirteen counties'. From Boston in the north, swinging round inland down to Cambridge in the south, an area of 1,200 square miles was now spread out like an apron-stage from the Wash, ready to become the setting for *our* history.

Springing forward in Time we pass the Stone Age and the Bronze Age until we consider for a moment the Roman occupation and the Dark Ages.

The needle on our time gauge moves rapidly across the face of the next five or six centuries, pausing just long enough for us to be reminded that whoever tried to occupy this part of East Anglia would always be faced with the same problem – what to do with the water collected in the lowlands, water below sea-level which would not flow uphill unaided. The Romans were aware that the value of this land could be increased if only it could be drained. So, just as they realized the need for good roads, they decided to construct canals. They cut long, deep dykes across the fields, strengthened the sea-banks against high tides, and introduced sluices in the rivers to help control the volume of water flowing into the Fens. Examples of their work can still be seen today, such as at Carr Dyke, near Northborough. 'Carr' is an old Norse word for a 'meadow recovered from a boggy marsh' and when the Romans finished their dyke it stretched from Waterbeach in Cambridgeshire to Witham in Lincolnshire. It is thought that they had a dual purpose for this waterway. It not only helped to drain the fields but it also provided their army with a further source of transport, enabling them to move legions of reinforcements quickly up to the north, especially to those areas where they had not yet built roads.

So it was under foreign rule, then, and later, that the shape of Britain began to change. Wastelands were turned into farms. Crops grew where there had only been infested waters, and communications were established by means of canal and highway. But, of course, the Roman occupation came to an end. The mighty army that had once marched triumphantly across their newly conquered territory was dispersed, its best soldiers called home to fight other campaigns, leaving little more than riff-raff behind to keep an eye on the surly natives. Corruption took over from the law, neglect followed efficiency, and sadly most of the work that had been achieved was left in ruins. Given that sort of opportunity nature soon takes over again and it was not long before the Fens were back to looking worse than they were four hundred years earlier. The area became a popular hideout for outlaws, terrorists and murderers. If civilization survived at all it did so in the growing number of religious settlements that were soon to be found in the Fens. By the eighth and ninth centuries these small communities – which had established themselves on what dry land they could find, i.e. the 'islands' of the fens – had become prosperous and influential places – Ely, Thorney, Ramsey, Sawtry, Peterborough and Crowland.

But still we must move on, to the next chapters of history which are just as intriguing. The Vikings soon put an end to the tranquillity of the monasteries. As the early historian Hugh Candidus of Peterborough Abbey was to record,

> Then came the Danes, servants of the Devil, and like mad dogs and robbers issuing of a sudden from their dens, even so they land of a sudden from their ships and come on the people that suspected no evil, burning cities, villas, young men, women and children ... All things they consume with robbery, fire and swords, taking care that none should live to bring tidings of this massacre.

I see a few expressions in the class now wondering, perhaps, if all this is relevant to the subject of literature. And it is. Each century has done something to change the ebb and flow of life in the Fens. Each age has contributed to the shape of the land and the kind of people we are. The moveable boundaries in Nature can be matched by the flux of historical events. One day the needle on time's gauge will pause for a moment at the twentieth century and we shall be little more than a sentence.

But let us stay for another minute with the geography of the Fens as much as the history. In many ways, of course, they cannot be separated. With a few quick sketches on the chalk-board we see how land was won, lost, reclaimed and lost again in the periods leading up to the seventeenth century when Sir Cornelius Vermuyden and The Gentlemen Adventurers arrived to 'drain the Fens for all time'. It was to be from this later period of our history that most of the literature was to come. Apart from Charles Kingsley's *Hereward the Wake*, with its evocative descriptions of the Fens, our books for the day are about events much nearer to our own time: Dorothy L. Sayers's

The Nine Tailors; L.P. Hartley's *The Brickfield* and *Facial Justice*; some essays by Hilaire Belloc and Graham Swift's novel *Waterland*. The aim of the course is to prove that the Fens have not been without their traditions, customs, legends and story-tellers. Nor have they been as devoid of literature as we were once led to believe. Indeed, it is surprising that they have not inspired more books than they have – especially when you realize how many good stories there are in collections such as W.H. Barrett's *Tales from the Fens*. In recent times it has been the film-maker who has come to appreciate the landscape's potential for dramatic settings. But as Graham Swift said in his foreword to my earlier book *The Spirit of the Fens* (1985), 'The Fens, once one's imagination has got to grips with them, are neither flat nor empty, nor are they to be consigned to the passive role of 'stage'. They have a character and drama of their own ... [They] are also compellingly and hauntingly strange.' So are we still waiting for our own great novelist, our own Thomas Hardy, Emily Brontë and even Dostoevsky?

iii

After our brief history lesson we begin to select some of those qualities that make this man-made landscape so compellingly and hauntingly strange. The words I hear most frequently are 'space', 'distance', 'sky', 'light', 'openness' and 'mysterious', seldom, if at all, 'flatness' or 'monotonous'.

'What I like most about the Fens,' says one, 'is that you can see so much land all at once, your vision is stretched.'

Another says, 'It's the space around me that I appreciate most after living in London. You've no idea what a thrill it is to see so much sky, to see the sun rise in the morning and set at night.'

'I like the people, too,' says another. 'They don't pretend to be what they're not and they seem so contented. There's none of this trying to keep up with the Joneses. You never hear them say, "Next door have just bought a new fridge or a telly, so we must get one now." You know where you are with them.'

One lady says what I am always pleased to hear. 'I like the light, not on a day like this admittedly, but on a good day there's something special about the light over the Fens. Perhaps it's something to do with the amount of water in the area – I mean, all those rivers and dykes, a whole network of waterways reflecting the sky. I think it's magical!'

Magical! Yes, it is a word you can associate with the Fens. It goes with 'haunting', 'mysterious' and 'compelling'.

But what of the literature that has come out of this 'magical' land? What of the writers who have tried to capture its elusiveness in their work? The students read out for me some of the excerpts I have selected for our study. Charles Kingsley, I fear, gets a rather tepid reception. He is seen as 'too wordy' or 'preachy', even 'too romantic' or 'too erudite'. Dorothy L. Sayers is more successful. Her descriptions of the landscape appeal more. 'They seem more personal, more genuinely felt,' says one.

> For instance, when she writes 'Mile after mile that flat road reeled away behind them. Here a windmill, there a solitary farmhouse, there a row of poplars strung along the edge of a reed-grown dyke,' that for me is what the Fens are like. And then we get "As they went, the land flattened more and more, if a flatter flatness were possible." I think she's got it perfectly.

Someone is tempted to disagree. 'I think it's still just clever writing. In my opinion nothing can match the real thing.'

As the day progresses we try to establish whether the literature does manage to convey the 'spirit of the place' or whether the landscape always defies the definitive description. Where does reality lie?

'But surely, in the novels we are concerned with more than the descriptions of the landscape? We should be more interested in the story,' says one of the teachers.

As usual there is a compromise. 'I agree that a novel's purpose is to tell a story but if it's set in a particular landscape I want to feel that I am there as well, so the descriptions have to be good – like Thomas Hardy's in *The Return of the Native*, for instance.'

So far, so good. Now L.P. Hartley begins to gain ground. Although the group find him rather 'distant' they concede that he is writing from personal experience, from the vivid memories of a child who spent some of his holidays with farming relatives in Crowland,

> We went to St. Botolph's Lodge two or three times a year, I

Here a windmill, there a solitary farmhouse

think; but it is Christmas that I remember best, just as I remember best the landscape frost-bound, with the tussocks of coarse grass that lined the dykesides, mop-heads white and stiff and bowed with their coating of rime, and the roads which normally had a muddy surface, brittle and crackling and striking sparks from the horses' hoofs.

The discussion is now relaxed, with many different opinions, much laughter, and ideas that are new to me. Outside, the fog gets a deeper shade of grey. Trees are shedding their own rain. For all we know the 'Ark' has floated away and we are locked in our cosy classroom until the dove returns with its sprig of olive.

During one of our break-times individuals begin to tell me some of their own anecdotes.

There used to be a chap come up from the Fen to do his shopping in the village and he always chained his bicycle to the railings in front of my grandfather's house, which didn't please him. So he said to the man the next time he came, 'How many times have you left your bike there?' And the man said, 'Just one more time than I have taken it away,' and went off to do his shopping.

'It's the sluices on the rivers, and the locks, that I find fascinating,' said another. 'They help to create such an atmosphere, especially on a day like this.'

Which brings us back to Graham Swift's *Waterland* whose story-teller 'lived in a fairy-tale place. In a lock-keeper's cottage, by a river, in the middle of the Fens. Far away from the wide world.' And that lock, and that story are to cast their own spell over our discussion for the rest of the afternoon.

Trying to sum up my own feelings about the Fens and their people I read my poem called 'Shadows',

Here, where the land cranes its thick neck
To stare beyond the water-line, we walk
On stilts to give our spirits height
And stride on legs which lift our weight
Above the reedy bog. You'd think
Such striving for the light would spunk
Our limbs to struggle for the sun
More eagerly than those whose bourn
Is half-way there. Not so!
We're frightened, too, of what we do not know.

More effort is required to keep
Our bodies raised. We need the cup
Of praising if we must look
At things of which we dare not speak.

Living below the level of the sea
Gives us the benefit of greater sky
In which to reach for light, but space
Can terrify and in our eyes
You'll see the fear of distances.
Yes, we are afraid of boundaries.
Safer to walk this land where clouds
Crouch on horizons, where clods
Glisten with ancient peat, soaked
By the rain. A man who's looked
Upon this land knows his own mind.
If we attempt to rise above the ground
It is to see with sharper eye
The contours of the earth. Maybe
We are afraid, not of the light or sun,
But of those shadows trying to get in.

iv

The day's last shadows were already upon us. It was nearly
half-past four and time to bring our one-day school to a close.
The hours have gone quickly. With expressions of satisfaction
and warm handshakes, the people I have been privileged to
share the day with begin to leave for home.

It has been a good way to spend a Saturday in February. In
our imaginations we have travelled all over the Fens, in every
season and into the past. We have enjoyed each other's company
and all those nervous beginnings at the start of the day have
been forgotten.

Outside we are back to reality. The shoppers and football
supporters are also making their ways home, looking as gloomy
as the dank evening itself. Perhaps they lost.

16   Making Sense of a Place

Everybody knows that one can increase what one has of knowledge or any other possession by going outwards and outwards; but what is also true, and what people know less, is that one can increase it by going inwards and inwards ...

Hilaire Belloc

Any landscape is a condition of the spirit

H.F. Amiel

It will be clear by now that I am grateful for what other writers have had to say about the Fens for through their eyes, which came but to look briefly, I have seen aspects of my native landscape that I might otherwise have missed. They have given that extra dimension to the familiar that wards off complacency.

Hilaire Belloc, for instance, had both a traveller's and a poet's eye for any place he visited, whether it was Italy, the Pyrenees, France, or the Fens. He loved mountains, a warm climate, and adventure. Yet he had a feeling for the fen country that is hardly surpassed and caught the nature of the landscape in many an original phrase, 'The Isle of Ely lying on the Fens is like a star-fish lying on a flat shore at low tide.' Or 'These dykes of the Fens are accursed things; they are the separation of friends and lovers ... The Fens are full of such tragedies.'

It was not uninformed descriptive writing either. He absorbed the history and customs of a place very quickly. In his essay 'A Family in the Fens' (from *Hills and the Sea*, 1906), he gave as concise an account of fen drainage and the Bedford family as you could wish to read. His healthy curiosity and enthusiasm caught the essence of the Fens splendidly and he knew what made this corner of England different, 'The infinite is always

161

well ahead of you and its symbol is the sky ... You may travel for the sake of great horizons, and travel all your life, and fill your memory with nothing but views from mountain-tops, and yet not have seen a tenth of the world.'

And that is something we have to remember about looking at the Fens. We only see a tenth of what they really are. I still think that one of the best commentators on our landscape was Charles Kingsley, the clergyman, historian and novelist, who was born in 1819 at Holne Vicarage near Dartmoor but came to know the Fens during his years at Cambridge, where he was an undergraduate at Magdalene College. In 1860, at the age of forty-one, he was to return to the university as Professor of Modern History, a chair he held for the next nine years. It was during this time that he wrote *Hereward the Wake* (1866), a novel which contains some of the best descriptions of the Fens. But his *Prose Idylls* (1884) was written in his retirement to the West Country and shows that he retained a deep love and understanding of the Fens, and the changes that had taken place.

> A certain sadness is pardonable to one who watches the destruction of a grand natural phenomenon, even though its destruction brings blessings to the human race. Reason and conscience tell us that it is right and good that the Great Fen should have become, instead of a waste and howling wilderness, a garden ... And yet the fancy may linger, without blame, over the shining mere, the golden reed-beds, the countless water-fowl, the strange and gaudy insects, the mystery, the majesty – for mystery and majesty there were – which haunted the deep Fens for many a hundred years. Little thinks the Scotsman, whirled down by the Great Northern Railway from Peterborough to Huntingdon, what a grand place, even twenty years ago, was that Holme and Whittlesea Mere, which is now a black, unsightly, steaming flat, from which the meres and reed-beds of the old world are gone, while the corn and the roots of the new world have not yet taken their place.

Change. It can never please everyone. Now, after more than two hundred years of intensive farming, which produced some of the best corn and root crops in Europe, the nature of the Fens is changing again. People who remember the great fields of wheat, potatoes, carrots and celery, will lament that their fertile land is slowly wasting away, that new housing estates and factories stand where crops once grew, and that one day nature may reclaim much that it once lost or even desert this corner of England altogether. Not only will the reed-beds and wildlife have gone, but the fields themselves. We belong to a time as well as a landscape.

ii

Sometimes I go to Ely for no other reason than to enjoy the train journey over the Fens. I have said before that it is still one of the best ways of getting a good first impression of the landscape's character. But it doesn't always work. I remember on one recent occasion when a fellow traveller, not from these parts, sat opposite me. After several minutes of looking out of the window he shook his head and said, 'God! What an ugly land this is. All muck and floods! How anyone can live out there beats me.'

Although my first reaction was to bristle at something I saw as an insult, I think I understood how he felt. In such a landscape what *can* you see unless you know what's hidden from the eye?

There are countries that can look back and remember a time when they were beautiful, their ruins reminders of days when palaces stood on their hills, when their halls resounded to the music of the harp or lute. Antiquity has been kind to them and, in their geographical setting, has left much for the rest of the world to admire.

Not here. Our modest landscape would only be able to recall a time of swamp and ague, when men shared winter with their animals, when dampness put a burden in the bone, when poverty was in their fires. I doubt if fenmen would have danced much then. They were more likely to have been tottering about on stilts through marsh and bog as they went from place to place, limping their way back home to dismal huts where peat smouldered on the hearth. Their music would have had a more primitive tune, nearer to a lament than a dance and would have had only the cold wind's accompaniment.

It would be true to say that today is the closest we have come to banquet halls and the pleasures of song. Since the drainage of the Fens, and with the skilled husbandry of farmers, life has improved enormously during the last hundred years. Now there are well lit, centrally heated houses (some finely built), and music rings out across the winter nights from village halls and church halls, as well as from pubs and discos. It is even possible to hear someone playing a piano in the front room of a house in the High Street, or (as we have seen) listen to a male voice choir entertaining in an old people's home, or perhaps someone still struggling to make a trombone sound tuneful. Some visitors to the Fens are even surprised to find so much culture and several creative artists from other parts of the country have now sought refuge here. One painter said to me, 'I feel closer to the elements here than I've felt anywhere and I can get on with my work without too many interruptions. I like the raw sense of history, too – you know, history unglamorized.'

But my fellow traveller on the the train would not have been as aware of the raw history that still lay hidden in that land which he found so ugly. Those countries, like Greece or Italy, may have preserved their past better simply because they had a more distinguished past in the first place. Most of our ruins lie beneath the soil, stripped bare of gods or myths. We have no ancient burial grounds to visit, no guarded tombs in which great kings faded from the earth – at least we have not found their equivalent yet, even though such important Bronze Age discoveries as those at Flag Fen, Peterborough have proved that there was a more civilized form of society here once than we thought. So far our relics are bog-oaks, prehistoric skeletons of animals and fish, broken pots and crude foundations covered more by mud than with golden masks or hieroglyphs. I wanted to say to the man opposite, it is only when you can imagine what is not visible that you begin to appreciate a landscape as vast and as secretive as the fens. But imagination, I've realized, is one of the quickest parts of the human mind to atrophy.

I could have tried to persuade him with,

> Look at where the plough has turned the furrows over for the next spring and you will notice tracks of a lighter soil where rivers once obeyed a natural flow before this land was drained. Those veins of silt (or rodhams as they're known) speak of a time when the Fens were wild with boar and bittern, wolves and geese. Beneath that earth which you now see as ugly is another world as old as anything you could find in Turkey or in Greece.

I could have given him Miller and Skertchly's *The Fenland, Past and Present* to read but he would have needed a much longer journey than the one from March to Ely. From that weighty

The parched grass shrunk back into the dykes

volume he would have learned about the Stone Folk and the Kelts, the Iceni tribes and Ancient Britons who first tried to cultivate this stubborn land. He would have read of the Roman and Danish years of occupation, of how this part of England was 'the last refuge' before the Norman Conquest,

The Fenland was, of all parts of Britain, one of the best suited for the last remnants, either of a vanquished nation, or of a vanquished political party, to hold out against their enemy till the last. There is reason to believe that some isolated spots in this wild region had been held by remnants of the old Keltic inhabitants for ages after East Anglia and Mercia had become English ground. It is even possible that, here and there, an outlying British settlement may have lingered on to the days of William, and that Hereward, as well as Eadric on the other side of England, may have found allies among the descendants of those whom his father displaced.

I could have called upon the same experts to confirm that the Fens do have their own beauty. Writing in 1878 they said,

We believe that the inhabitants of the Fens – at the present-day – enjoy as many sunny skies, as many beautiful star-lit nights, and as magnificent cloudscapes as any people in England ... The beauty of the sky is becoming proverbial. The breadth of view here presented to the spectator – embracing as it does the concavity of an almost perfect hemisphere, enables him to see the whole cloud formation and to watch uninterruptedly all the changing variety of its form, colour, or motion.

But I still do not think I could have converted this unimpressed visitor on a day when the Fens wore winter's frown with such stubborn determination. Nor is it always easy to convince fen-dwellers themselves of the land's hidden beauty or of its historical significance, especially in winter when the surface can look 'all muck and floods'. Sometimes the past refuses to speak and Nature herself is disinclined to co-operate. On certain days the land can look mean, pinched by the wind, its blood thin in the furrows, the parched grass shrunk back into the dykes where frost waits to suck it dry. Then the fields' backs are hunched against the sky, their old tracks as grey as remembered scars, the twisted headlands like arthritic hands wringing themselves in front of a stingy fire. On such a day even the setting sun looks miserly, unwilling to radiate one comforting ray through the dead cinders of cloud. I feel like repeating what the passenger on the train said, 'How anyone can live out there, beats me!' Such greyness chills the most ardent lover of the Fens. Houses stay crouched low to the ground. Farms wither into shadows. Earth goes into mourning. But for how long? Such days are only part of a season and make the opposites even more acceptable. How foolish to judge a landscape or a season in one day.

I have made this journey to Ely so often that I feel I ought to make better use of the time, if only to catch up on reading, or at least attempt the daily crossword. But by the time the train has reached Whittlesey I find myself compelled to look out of the windows again, and even then I am torn as to which side of the train I should be sitting to get the best of the landscape. We should never grow tired of the familiar for it, too, can surprise. Beyond Whittlesey the simple choice between left and right now becomes a dilemma. I want to see both aspects because the views are never twice the same. The light may be different. The fields on one side may have been ploughed and the others not. Even in winter the mood can vary by the hour as well as the week. This was the railway line on which we travelled as children when being taken to the Norfolk coast for our annual holidays. I know the route backwards. Sometimes, on a December day those long-ago summers can suddenly flash up on to the memory-screen and for a tempting moment transform the winter landscape into the hazy heat of summer. Beyond March the decision becomes even more difficult because there will now be the Welney Washlands either side of the track as well as the farms. Within a month I have made four separate journeys and they have compressed the four seasons into as many days. If, out of those days, I could choose only one to represent the true spirit of the Fens, which would it be? It is a futile exercise for, as I have said, you cannot possibly select just one day to do justice to the other 364. It is enough for me to be amazed at the landscape on any day. My eyes never weary of the flatness, blackness, distance, or vagaries of the season's weather. It is a journey I do not wish to end and I am always sorry to see the imposing outline of Ely Cathedral coming into view as the train turns towards the city. Such a journey must mean more to me than a stranger for beneath the deceptive surface of that landscape I see centuries and might also be able to glimpse that which is to come when what I praise now no longer exists. For change there will be.

iii

What do we take with us when we can no longer be part of a place? What do we remember of a house that is no longer ours? And what of a landscape will always be part of the mind's geography when the miles that separate are too many for us to get back? Some people can throw off a place like discarding an old coat, they can walk away from a house like throwing away an unwanted pair of shoes – and perhaps with justification, for landscapes can hurt too. Why should everyone feel attached to somewhere, or have an affection for a place where they did not want to be? I have known many people whose jobs forced them to live in the Fens, sometimes for years, but they could never grow to like them. It was somewhere to live while there was work to be done and when the time came to leave there was no weeping. Any feeling of 'belonging' to a place is unacceptable to some, and too deep an affection for the past is unhealthy to others. A friend who could be at home anywhere, once said to me, 'Why dwell so much in the past? We can only go forward and should therefore be more concerned about tomorrow than yesterday.' I argued that it was not indulging in nostalgia to be aware of the past. Rather than shedding the past like a worn-out coat you should put it on, or carry it with you as part of the future. It helped to shape us, had some influence on the kind of people we are, so why disown it as some worthless thing of which we are ashamed? Every journey has a beginning. You cannot start from now because the present itself quickly becomes past. And who wants to come from nowhere, or leave nothing behind?

Over the years that I have been writing about the Fens I think I have found that, broadly speaking, people fit into one of two main categories – those for whom 'belonging' to a place means everything, and those for whom 'anywhere will do' as long as you're with your family. Neither attitude makes either person less attractive. It depends on the kind of person you are. If you have moved around since childhood it must be difficult to know where your roots are. Those roots are not necessarily where you were born. They may not even be in the place to which you were transplanted. They may not even exist. Quoting from my friend again, 'You are where you are, wherever the wind may blow you, sticking to the side of a wall for a little while before being blown somewhere else.'

Dandelion seeds? Accidents? Shadows, or part of some ancient spring without whose nourishment we would perish should it run dry? Perhaps it is a good thing that we are all so different. And, in defence of the Fens, I must also say that I have known people come to them for what they thought would be no more than three or four years and they have stayed for forty.

But, in the end, I can only speak personally, and what I know is that my landscape has been such an integral part of the whole of my life so far that it will always be with me wherever I go. The light will always last even in darkness. A man will be ploughing still, though his tractor vanish in mist and the attendant gulls are forever lost in the furrows turned long ago. Beyond the rich, black fields where clouds are torn by rain, will always be part of a sky where affection shines through the cold eye of winter. And there will be no nostalgia or regret, only gratitude.

iv

And so my day in Ely came to an end. And no, I have not said anything about the city itself, or its great cathedral. I could add nothing to what has already been said. I went for the journey rather than for the place. The rhythm of the train helps me to think and someone else has to worry about the driving.

My journey home was taken in the dark. I could only imagine now the flooded washlands, the wayside stations, the farmhouses hidden somewhere out there in the night, the people I had met sitting by their own fires. And I was content to let my memories of them fill up my travelling time. I had a book to read but it no longer interested me. I had someone sitting opposite but we did not speak. Our brightly lit *Sprinter* rattled across the Fens and it was like being in a time capsule.

Should anyone ask me what I have been doing during these winter months I think I should have to say, 'I have been trying to make sense of a place, to persuade others to see a little of what I see.' But what is it about this place that compels me to go on writing about it, even when there are times when I would like to be writing about something, or somewhere, else? Maybe I am still searching for the answer, for the one phrase that will sum it all up and leave me satisfied.

But the answer, like the landscape itself, is evasive, for the clues are always changing with the days. Each time I go into the Fens they look different. I feel like a portrait painter whose subject will not sit still. So I persist, pursuing the elusive description and still failing to explain why this passion has lasted so many years. Is it no more than a natural loyalty to one's native roots? I believe it goes beyond loyalty for often loyalty excludes criticism and the existence of faults. I am aware of the Fens' shortcomings, that in purely physical terms they cannot be compared with the more obvious beauty of, say, the Lake District or Devon. But the features they have are their own and trying to get away from them is like trying to escape one's shadow, to disown the image in the mirror. I'm stuck with them, and they with me. If ever I make sense of this prolonged affair the Fens will, I am sure, have lost their appeal and their haunting spaces will have nothing but emptiness. And who wants to be in love with a void?

> You can hate these roads or find, like hills,
> They lift you, step by step, out of the soul's drought.

17 Farewell to the Swans

To everything there is a season, and a time to every purpose under the heaven.

Ecclesiastes

In its own limited, austere and almost grudging fashion the Fen acknowledged the return of the sun. The floods withdrew from the pastures; the wheat lifted its pale green spears more sturdily from the black soil.

Dorothy L. Sayers

i

As this book began with the arrival of the swans at the Welney Wetlands it is appropriate that it should end with their departure. With their going the winter season will also be over and we shall be eager for the longer days of spring. But there will be an air of sadness when that moment comes – sadness and satisfaction, rather like coming to the end of a good book or a moving play. The drama, spectacle, beauty and poetry all have to finish but we hope that something will remain in the memory to prolong our joy.

As I write now the swans have not yet departed but I have been back to the centre to find out from Don Revett what it feels like when they do decide that the time has come to return to their summer breeding-grounds in northern Russia and Iceland. I think the expression in his eyes said,

How does anyone feel when a whole family leaves home? We know they have to go, we know that most of them will be back next November, but you can't help feeling the wrench. After all, they have been with us for nearly four months and you get used to them. Because of their daily timetable they become part of

171

your everyday life. You know their habits and get used to their noise. Then one morning you go over to the hides and it's all quiet and you realize they've gone. You just stand there looking at the empty water and it takes a little time to adjust.

I asked Don if, as most of the swans arrived at the washlands in the dark, whether they left in the same way?

Not necessarily, they don't need to. Quite a lot of them leave at dawn, or early daylight. You can tell when they're preparing to go. You see them craning their necks and sniffing the air. They're checking on the wind directions and weather-fronts, trying to establish if conditions are favourable for the flight home. They won't go until they're ready. Sometimes, because the weather itself can be so unpredictable, they make an error and leave when they think it's all right, only to find by the time they get to Holland the weather has changed dramatically, so they turn round and come back, knowing that they probably need a few more weeks' feeding before things improve.

Remembering how the swallows and martins prepared themselves for their long journeys in the autumn, I asked if the swans went into some kind of training ready for their flights. Certainly during their stay in England they would not have had much exercise, apart from going backwards and forwards from feeding-grounds to roosting on the water.

Yes, you notice them getting organized. They start flying in formation and going further afield. You see certain swans with initiative taking up the lead position in the V-formation. They won't always keep that position for the whole flight home. They take it in turns. The front bird has all the hard work to do. When they finally leave, they rise and circle over the water and appear to be going in the opposite direction to the one they want. Then they fly higher, taking an even wider circle, and swing round as if in a final salute of farewell. Sometimes you don't even see that much, they have already gone.

Because the winter of 1992/93 had been such a wet one I wondered whether this had been in the birds' favour, rather than one which might have been bitterly cold?

It can be too cold and it can be too wet. It's not much fun for them if it's a hard winter and the water is frozen over for a couple of weeks. It might be all right for the skaters but not the birds.

This has certainly been one of the most prolonged winters of flooding that I can remember here. Not only have the washlands been under an excess of water, but also the feeding-grounds. The swans can't go without food for too long so they take off and look for somewhere else where it's a bit drier. They'll probably go down to the West Country for three weeks and then come back. Birds will always find a habitat. I remember once, a few years back, we built a sand wall into one of the banks and it wasn't long before the martins found it and made it their home.

What about winds? We've had a lot of strong winds this winter too. They must be a disadvantage, especially for big birds?

True. You can imagine the energy and power a swan needs to fly. With a wing-span like theirs a gale is the last thing they want. Personally I find the winds out here more depressing than the wet. Day after day of howling wind gets you down. You feel so battered. But, when it stops, the peace is wonderful.

In a job like this you must have a philosophy of sorts, a belief in what you are doing; so what motivates you during the winter months when the weather can be so inhospitable? It's more than a job, isn't it?

I suppose it is. I love wildlife and want to protect it. I'm here for several reasons – to look after the birds, to provide a centre of interest for the public, to make people as happy and as comfortable as I can without disturbing the birds. One of the main problems is in keeping the right balance between the enterprise and the purpose for it being here. It's like a narrow margin between a private world, which is the birds', and the public world brought in by visitors. You have to control it as gently as you can. If too many people are out in the hides at a time they could disturb the birds and they would just disappear, which is not very helpful as the people have come to see the birds. But we need as many members and visitors as we can get to keep the place going, so where do you draw the line? I think one of our important roles here is to educate the public, especially children, in the wonders of the natural world, which is why we like to see families here at the weekends.

The hides can be a bit overcrowded at times and I wondered whether the Wildfowl Trust had any plans for extending its facilities. 'Yes. We'd like to enlarge the members' observation room and put an extra wing on the hides, but it's an expensive project and at the moment there's not that sort of money about. But who knows?'

Behind the shrug of his shoulders was perhaps the hope that some wealthy philanthropist would suddenly become interested in wild-fowl and do something. I can now understand why so many people are so enthusiastic, not only for the different species of swans but for all the other birds to be found there as well, the pintails, shovelers, mallards, pochards, wigeon and teals. And beyond the wetlands themselves are the resident fenland birds and the history of the Fens as well.

Before my meeting with Don Revett I had called in again at The Lamb and Flag in Welney, surprised to find on a Tuesday lunch-time that the place was full and every table occupied. Within seconds I could see they were all bird-watchers, studying their books, comparing notes, pondering over whether they had seen a certain species or not. Some had already been out to the hides, others were on their way. They sat in groups round the blazing fire, stepping over the two large sleeping dogs as they made their way back from the bar, and each one engrossed in the subject of birds. I couldn't help feeling that the Welney Centre was going to retain its popularity for many more winters.

As I drove home later that afternoon a low, weak sun made the extensive floodwater gleam. The fields now took on 'such a form as Grecian goldsmiths make / Of hammered gold and gold enamelling'. Gnarled willows standing in several inches of water now had mirror images. In the distance there was no horizon for the mist had already edged its way across the Fens, giving the landscape that special quiet, subtle, eerie and mysterious character that can only be found in this part of England. Even the pylons appeared to be watching and waiting as they stood like herons across the margins of the land.

I was not sure whether I would be back to see the actual departure of the swans, unless that event took place within the next two weeks. It was possible that this book would be on its way to the publishers by the time the birds decided to leave. So this journey home was to be my own farewell, my own sad leave-taking – at least for a time. I knew that next autumn I would be back to see the whole splendid season start again. In the meantime I can only wonder with the poet W.B. Yeats,

Amongst what rushes will they build ...

Among what rushes will they build,
By what lake's edge or pool
Delight men's eyes when I awake some day
To find they have flown away.

ii

But it is more than the swans that will soon be gone, it is a winter
that has been made very different for me by the many meetings I
have had with people I had not met before and who, because of
their experiences, memories, warmth of friendship and
willingness to talk, have made me more aware of the Fens'
uniqueness, pride, and irresistible appeal.

I have also appreciated more the peace of the winter Fens.
Not that you cannot find peace in the other seasons. In my
earlier volume, *Call it a Summer Country* (1978), I wrote about
being out on the Gedney Marshes in July and was clearly
enthusiastic about it then,

> You become aware of the stillness, the beautiful quietness of a
> summer's day in an almost primeval landscape; not silence,

because the sweet humming wind can be heard combing the grass. Today there are no jet-planes flashing low over the marsh, not even skylarks. The peace is unbelievable. Soak it up, drink it, absorb it into every cell of your body.

I am not sure that you could these days. Summers do not seem as quiet and peaceful as they were fifteen years ago. There is much more traffic in the Fens now and there has been a considerable increase in building. Where once there were fields which I never thought would disappear are now housing-estates. What were footpaths are now metalled roads. But there is still something different about the peace to be found in winter. The stillness is more intense, less languorous than on a summer's day. It has the kind of expectancy you can sometimes feel in an empty church, or a silent room where you wait for someone to return home. It is, I believe, a deeper peace, one which I have experienced many times during those shorter, uncrowded days, and especially in the afternoons when the land looks deserted.

Where are these quiet places? Some, you will understand, I must always keep secret. But there are others – certain river-banks and dykesides where I can enjoy a favourite vista. I like to be near water, or the memory of water, which is such an integral part of the Fens. The site of Whittlesea Mere often calls me back to stand where its shores were, to imagine the great gatherings it knew, both summer and winter. In wintertime the water could cover as much as 3,000 acres, providing a lake the size of Derwent Water. And, if it was a hard winter with plenty of frosts, the Mere became a meeting place for skaters, not just a few but thousands. Just as it had its summer regattas, so it had its ice fairs when the shores were lined with booths selling hot sausages, pork pies, roast chestnuts and liquor. There were punters and fortune-tellers, children on sledges and men 'sailing' ice-boats. Skilled skaters arrived from all over the Fens and beyond to compete for a trophy or prize-money. Others entered events which could win them the prize of a pig, a leg of mutton, or a large loaf of bread. Adam Sedwick, writing on 30 January 1841, said 'I went to Whittlesea and saw thousands and I think tens of thousands whirling on the ice. There were certainly 10,000 persons assembled one day on Whittlesea Mere to see a match – another day nearly as many.'

All these scenes came to an end in 1851 when the Mere was drained and you are probably wondering why I would choose such a scene as one of my quiet places. I wouldn't if the Mere still existed because I don't like crowds and, apart from a brief glimpse of the spectacle I would walk away. But now there are only ghosts and the silent echoes of what it was once, I can enjoy its memories. It has become, I suppose, a symbol of what the whole fen country was before everything was changed.

It is the same with Adventurers' Fen from Swaffham Prior to Upware. This land once belonged to The Gentlemen Adventurers who put up most of the money for Vermuyden's drainage schemes, but the delays in achieving the expected results and the distribution of drained land caused bitter resentment. The new land was farmed but, as the years passed, the farms were neglected and after several wet winters it was reclaimed by nature, to become once again a large mere. It remained so until the War Agricultural Committee decided to have it drained again in the Second World War to give farmers more land for the extra food the country needed to grow. Before then it had been an area much loved by James Wentworth Day, who described it as, 'a wild and lovely place (which) dwells in memory as a very perfect picture of the older England, the England of Hereward the Wake and St Guthlac'. Not that the gentle saint of Crowland would have approved of Mr Wentworth Day's passion for shooting. Before the war thousands of birds were shot each year in this part of the Fens – teals, widgeons, shovelers, pochards, geese, pheasants and sometimes swans. Writing in 1938 of 'this barbarous century' he must have overlooked the days when the air vibrated with the sound of 12-bores and punt-guns as they volleyed round after round over the waters, bagging, as William Kent claims to have done, '160 widgeon with six shots one bitter day on the washes at Mepal'. Now we lament that some birds, such as the marsh-harrier and bittern are either rare or extinct.

Nevertheless, in his book *A History of the Fens* (1954), Mr Wentworth Day was able to write his own eloquent elegy for his lost mere,

> Then came the war. They drained the fen with a great clamour of bureaucratic self-praise. The waters went away and the fish died by the cart-load ... They set fire to the reeds, and for a day

or more my secret Fen roared and crackled in a tawny yellow, red-hot sea of flame ... The duck rose up and fled on whimpering wings. The moorhens and the rails, the bittern and the warblers went, no man knows whither. Perhaps they, like the reeds, were suffocated and burned in that unholy holocaust. The Place of Gulls was a sea of sinking ashes ... An insult to the high Fen skies. An altar of burned beauty. A sacrifice to man's neglect of pre-war farming ... thus, in a funeral pyre vanished the last and loveliest remnant of what had been a recreation in all its wild glory.

Nature gives and nature takes. The expense of draining the mere, and making it into arable land again, cost the Country Agricultural Executive Committees at the time something 'in the neighbourhood of £25,000,000 a year. Do the Committees grow £25,000,000's worth of food each year?' asked Mr Wentworth Day. 'The answer, I think, is no!' Such extravagance, he felt, was destroying the beauty of the English countryside, our 'heritage of birds and beasts' and was now 'killing the spirit, the soul, and the independence of the countryman'.

I suppose we all have our own ideas of beauty and I find great satisfaction in driving along that cracked, narrow road over Adventurers' Fen with its rich, shining black soil and generous crops. It is a blessing to the eye and the spirit. I prefer to see growth. The irony of it now is that we have too much land, that the fen soil grows too well. Crops for which the land was created are no longer wanted in such quantities, for reasons given in some of my previous chapters. Perhaps one day the waters will take back what they believe to be theirs.

As much as I enjoy the journey from Swaffham Prior to Upware, I am always at my happiest when I get back to the heart of the Black Fens. From Adventurers' Fen and its single-track, pot-holed road, I made my way to Stretham, then to Witchford and Coveney, neither of which has anything to do with witches. The name 'Coveney' is believed to come from an earlier description as 'a bay in the Isle'. From Coveney to Pymore the heartbeat of the Fens is felt more strongly. The high road gives splendid panoramas of the land below and the ancient smell of peat is back. In the early afternoon light there was a bloom on the fields as the first layers of mist hovered over the land. From Pymore to Welney the pulse grew even more strong, as it does when you get closer to home. Hundreds of swans were grazing in the fields away from the floods. From Welney to Manea, alongside acres of daffodils already in bud, I was reminded of how farming is having to adapt to the market and EC regulations. I still can't get used to seeing bulb crops in the Fens where I expect to see potatoes and sugar-beet. But more and more bulbs are being grown in Cambridgeshire, which can't please the bulb-growers in Lincolnshire. Does anyone win?

On the horizon, or where the horizon should be, the two-car sprinter train I so often use for my journeys to Ely and Norwich inched itself along the track like a caterpillar on a branch. I paused to watch it pass, then drove on to Wimblington, Benwick and Whittlesey – a world I have known all my life and still find appealing. The space, the light, the stillness. It is then that you can wrap the atmosphere of the Fens around you like a cloak, or as my friend Phil Gray the wild-fowler once said to me, 'You put the Fens on like a favourite coat, and when you do you feel you're at home.'

I think I might even be disappointed when summer comes and the fields are busy, when the roads are dusty and more travelled on, when the sun prolongs the dry days and sets inconspicuously beyond the horizon, no longer veiled in mist or broken by the flight of swans returning to their roosting place.

iii

I can't help thinking of a year ago, of February 1992, when I experienced a winter of a very different kind. I was in Russia, in frozen snow and temperatures of 20°F below zero. The long journey from St Petersburg to Moscow, across that vast landscape of birch forests and white plains, made me realize how small the Fens are in comparison. I was reminded of that visit especially when I first began writing this book and stood out on the Hundred Foot Washes watching some of the swans arriving from Siberia. I thought of that cold day when I had visited the prison in St Petersburgh where, in 1849, the great writer Fyodor Dostoevsky was kept in solitary confinement for eight months awaiting trial for his part in helping to promote a progressive socialist party. On 22 December, at the age of twenty-eight, he was taken from his cell, blindfolded and tied to a post on the parade square, ready to face the firing-squad. The soldiers rifles were already aimed and ready-cocked for the

execution when, at the closest second to death, a reprieve came
through and Dostoevsky's sentence was changed to four years
of hard labour in Siberia, to be followed by five years in the
Army. As chilling as my visit to that prison was I was even more
moved when I was taken to the apartment at No. 5 Kuznechny
Perenlok, on the corner of a street now named after the author
but which, in his day, was known as Yamskay Street. I slid and
stumbled my way through the snow, trying to keep up with my
guide. Along the pavements were dozens of middle-aged
women who were trying to sell, or barter, something – half a
dozen eggs, a cucumber, a home-made cake, a woollen scarf,
some old china plates, anything that might get them a few
copeks to help buy what they needed. When we entered the
apartment it was more like entering a shrine. The attendants
spoke in whispers. A few other visitors walked around on tiptoe.
In the entrance hall were the writer's walking-sticks, his
umbrella and his hat. From the hall we stepped into the
children's room. The guide still spoke in whispers, 'This is where
he told his children stories and taught them to write ...
sometimes they would push a note under his study door when he
was working, asking if they could have a sweet.' We then moved
into the dining room where Dostoevsky had entertained many
of his literary friends, some famous, some now forgotten. Then
we finally stood at the door of his study where he had written his
last great novels, often working through the night and going to
bed at 5 a.m. Everything was still in place, just as it had been on
the day he died – the beautiful wooden desk, his bookcase, the
sofa on which he slept, the glass of strong tea, even the doctor's
prescription that arrived too late that January morning to save
the author's life for another few weeks. The demanding creative
life he had imposed upon himself, the lung disease that had
troubled him ever since his imprisonment in Siberia, and a fatal
throat haemorrhage, finally ended his courageous and
productive life. He died 28 January 1881, at the age of sixty.

And what on earth has all this got to do with the fen-country?
Simply that the swans brought something of that man and his
landscape with them to Welney. Moved as I was by their flight
and by their calls of joy at the end of so long a journey, I took
shelter in one of the hides and wrote a poem which I called
'*Dostoevsky and the Swans*',

They fly in with the cries of a lonely Russian
Whose longing often looked at their free wings
As they left a Siberian plain for the warmer air
Of an English winter. They brighten our skies
With whiteness lit by November's sun, leaving him
In his bare landscape, carving his songs
In the grey ice of a prison. No landfall or star
Will ever bring him to these waters. The swans come
Bearing his tired soul wrapped in a dream of Spring,
His voice caught in their flight, in the proud light
Of eyes that have travelled over more than a Continent.
Whatever snow smothered his footsteps or frost made numb,
They will return and he will hear in the night
Their cries of longing that will bring them home.

And tomorrow, or a few weeks later, somewhere in Russia someone will be waiting for *their* swans to return. I hope the arrival of those tired white wings, and the sound of those familiar cries, will give them that moment of excitement, the same thrill, that they gave us. At least nature will have kept her word.

With February gone and daffodils in bloom

iv

But does she? With February gone and daffodils already in full bloom, we ought to be able to say with some confidence that winter is over. Not so. March has arrived in a pageantry of snow-showers and sunlight, followed by cold winds from the north-east which have put an Arctic edge on the day. Slowly the world outside fills with a new and unexpected whiteness. Trees, hedges and gardens are transformed, the sky now as solemn as a funeral director. It is as if the past four months have been buried, as if they had never been. It is as if winter is only just about to begin, leaving me with the uncomfortable feeling that I, too, should start again.

Select Bibliography

Astbury, A.K., *The Black Fens* (Golden Head, 1958)
Belloc, Hilaire, *Hills and the Sea* (Methuen, 1906)
Clare, John, *The Poems* (Dent, 1935)
Collis, J. Stewart, *The Vision and the Glory* (Knight, 1972)
——, *The Worm Forgives the Plough* (Knight, 1973)
Darby, H.C., *The Drainage of the Fens* (CUP, 1940)
Hartley, L.P., *The Brickfield* (Hamilton, 1964)
Heathcote, J.M., *Reminiscences of Fen & Mere* (Longmans, 1876)
Howat, Polly, *Ghosts & Legends of Lincolnshire & the Fens* (Countryside Books, 1992)
Kilvert, Francis, *Kilvert's Diary 1870–79* (Cape, 1944)
Kingsley, Charles, *Alton Locke* (Macmillan, 1851)
——, *Hereward the Wake* (Macmillan, 1866)
——, *Prose Idylls* (Macmillan, 1882)
Miller & Skertchly, *The Fenland Past & Present* (Longmans, 1878)
Sayers, Dorothy L., *The Nine Tailors* (Gollancz, 1934)
Storey, Edward, *Portrait of the Fen-country* (Hale, 1971)
——, *Call it a Summer Country* (Hale, 1978)
——, *Fen Boy First* (Hale, 1978)
Swift, Graham, *Waterland* (Heinemann, 1983)
Wentworth Day, J., *A History of the Fens* (Harrap, 1954)
Woodforde, James, *The Diary of a Country Parson* (OUP, 1935)

Index